HARD BARGAIN

HARD BARGAIN

Transforming Public Sector Labour-Management Relations

Peter Warrian

McGilligan Books

© copyright Peter Warrian 1996

Editor:	Ann Decter
Copy editor:	Angela Hryniuk
Cover design:	Denise Maxwell
Cover photograph:	David Hartman
Layout:	Heather Guylar

All rights reserved. No part of this book may be used or reproduced in any manner whatsoever without written permission except in the case of brief quotations embodied in critical articles and reviews. For information address McGilligan Books, P.O. Box 16024, 859 Dundas Street West, Toronto, Ontario, Canada M6J 1W0.

Canadian Cataloguing in Publication Data

Warrian, Peter
 Hard bargaining : transforming public sector labour-management relations

Includes bibliographical references.
ISBN 0-9698064-3-4

1. Employee-management relations in government — Canada.
2. Employee-management relations in government.
3. Collective bargaining — Government employees — Canada.
4. Collective bargaining — Government. I. Title.

HD8005.6.C3W37 1996   331.041350000971   C96-931699-2

Printed and bound in Canada by union labour.

To Margret, for her calming influence

CONTENTS

Acknowledgements 9

INTRODUCTION — Transformation or Exit: Public Sector Labour-Management Relations in the 1990s 11
    Cuts and Contracting Out at the Union Hall. 12
    A New Public Sector Management Model 12
    Strikes and Contracting Out: OPSEU and GM, 1996 15
    Hard Bargaining in a New Environment 19

CHAPTER 1 — A System in Crisis 21
    Public Sector Wagnerism 21
    A New Understanding of Public Sector Employment Relations.... 27
    The Traditional Concept of Public Sector and Private Sector Differences.. 36
    The Ghost in Public Sector Bargaining....................... 44
    Business Process Re-engineering and Wagnerism 46
    The Beginning of the End or the End of the Beginning? 48

CHAPTER 2 — The New Managerialism......................... 49
    The Drivers of Change 49
    New Public Management Globally 50
    The Roots of Change 51
    The Debate on NPM: Passing Fad or Real Change? 55
    Public Sector Reform: A Look at Some Results 59
    Linking Measurement and Management...................... 66
    Macro-Level Performance Indicators 68
    Performance-based Challenges to Labour-Management Relations.. 71
    "De-Inventing Government" — New Zealand Comes to Alberta .. 72
    Labour-Management Relations and the Contract State 75
    The Purchaser-Provider Split and Labour-Management Relations.. 77
    Employment Relations and Re-Engineering Delivery Systems 78

CHAPTER 3 — Fad, Phase or Future? Managerialism in Health Care . 83
    Lessons from Britain's National Health Service 84
    The Ontario Public Health System 87
    Sunnybrook Health Science Centre: A Model for Multi-Skilling... 94

Performance Indicators in Action: Redcliffe Hospital, Queensland, Australia 98
The Failure of Conventional Productivity Measurement for Public Sector Services. 100
Managerialism in Health Care: Promises, Realities and Labour-Management Relations. 101

CHAPTER 4 — Evolution or Devolution? Municipal Service Reform . . . 105
Municipal Labour-Management Relations: Bargaining in a Fish Bowl 105
Reduced Transfer Payments — A New Service Environment. 107
Service Reform Trends Internationally 109
Contracting Out: Theory vs. Practice. 111
Ontario's Municipal Support Program: A Test Site for NPM 114
Municipal Planning for Performance: Sunneyvale, California 115
Re-engineering Service Delivery: Metro Toronto Social Services Division 116
The New Paradigm and Municipal Labour-Management Relations . 126

CHAPTER 5 — Ontario Hydro: Toward Participatory Change 131
Employees, Bargaining Units and Bargaining Agents 132
The Costs of Transformation 133
PWU on Decentralization: A Participatory Proposal 140
The Costs of Unemployment: Rational Insistence on Job Security . 142
Restructuring Potential: Revamping Human Resource Management 144
Restructuring Lessons: Electricity Commission of New South Wales. 146
Sector Model of Adjustment. 147

CHAPTER 6 — Hard Changes, New Bargains: Transforming Public Sector Labour-Management Relations 153
Trade Unions and Employee Involvement 155
Bargaining Strategically in the Public Sector 158
Public Sector Innovation. 162
New Economic Assumptions 165
Toward a New Economics of Collective Bargaining 167
Strategies for a New Era. 168
Hard Economic Bargains 171

Appendices 173
Glossary 191
References 199

ACKNOWLEDGEMENTS

On completing a manuscript, the author is most aware of the things still left unsaid or said less well than originally hoped. What stands out in even bolder relief is one's debt to friends and commentators. Much thanks to Peter Burton, Peter Cameron, David Black, Bob Hebdon, Heather McAllister, John O'Grady and Michael Trebilcock in Canada; Carol Haddad, Arie Halachmi and Mark Holzer in the USA; Guy Callender and Judy Johnston in Australia. Finally to my editor the unflappable Ann Decter and researchers Jordan Berger and Tim Lewis.

— INTRODUCTION —
TRANSFORMATION OR EXIT:
Public Sector Labour-Management Relations in the 1990s

In January 1996, the fate of two dozen Calgary laundry workers represented by the Canadian Union of Public Employees (CUPE) galvanized Alberta public opinion, forcing Ralph Klein's government to pause in its previously unstoppable campaign to restructure the Alberta health care system. The unfairness of low-wage women and racial minority workers reduced to poverty-level wages, then dismissed from their jobs, outweighed the presumed necessity of balancing the budget and "improving" public services by turning them over to private contractors. The Alberta premier blinked because justice and employment rights are basic expectations in political democracies. Even populist governments have their limits.

A month later, hard on the heels of 120,000 labour and social protesters demonstrating in Hamilton, Ontario against draconian cuts announced by the Harris government, the Ontario Public Service Employees Union (OPSEU) also struck. Its 65,000 Ontario civil service members went on strike over employee seniority rights and severance entitlements in the face of the government's announcement of 13,000-26,000 pending layoffs. The cuts amount to between twenty and thirty-five per cent of OPSEU's membership in the Ontario civil service.

Why here, why now? Are these public sector labour clashes the result of the macho right-wing policies of Premiers' Klein and Harris or are they directly tied to necessary government debt and deficit reduction? Is it simply another spin of the political cycle — right-wing governments replacing liberal and left-wing governments — the perennial swing of the political spectrum from right to left to right?

It is none of the above. These events are rooted in broad-based changes in the financing, administration and management of public service delivery combined with an outmoded model of labour-management relations transposed from the private sector mass production industries. The public sector is the most highly unionized segment of the economy, eighty-five percent (85%) of legally eligible employees have legal bargaining agents and agreements. Obviously, there can be no solution to the question of how public services should be delivered and at what cost, without a solution to the labour-management issue.

Cuts and Contracting Out at the Union Hall

When union reps and management hear their daily diet of "C&C" — cuts and contracting out — in the media, they know they can look forward to another stressful but predictable day. The unionist knows exactly what to expect and what to do. The picket signs and the grievance forms are pre-formatted and ready to go. Their management counterparts are equally busy dusting off their standard budget and concessions speech: on the basis of a cursory and largely irrelevant page and a half memo on costs, union members' contract rights are to be rolled back. Both parties go into negotiations knowing that they will win a few, lose a few, and settle in the middle on the rest. It is a stressful, conflict-filled environment, but it is also, ironically, totally predictable. Everyone knows what to do, everyone knows what the rules are. The message is — this is a stable labour-management relations environment. What happens when the message changes? What do they do when the world turns upside down, and the old rules no longer apply?

A New Public Sector Management Model

The message has altered, and the shift is one that will fundamentally destabilize the traditional public sector labour-management system. What is happening is more than the imposition of major budget cuts, because that alone would not destabilize a labour-management system built up over fifty years of give and take. Nor will massive contracting out solve all of the government's problems as employer. And, the change is more than the importation of popular new management techniques from the private sector, such as total quality management (TQM).

A distinctive new public sector management model is emerging for the management of public services as a whole. Public service delivery is being disaggregated — pulled apart — as services themselves are split off from their financing and policy direction. Much will be contracted out, and more often, contracted to new organizations. As a result, public sector labour and management will face each other in new ways. What is spinning people's heads is the emergence of a whole new model for public sector management. This is a broad trend, with local variations, across all industrialized economies.

Common Core Of New Public Management (NPM)

- Cost cutting and greater accountability
- Disaggregating bureaucracies into separate agencies
- Decentralization of management authority
- Purchasing services split from providing them
- Market and quasi-market mechanisms
- Performance targets, indicators and output objectives
- Tenure and standard salaries replaced by contracts, pay related to performance (PRP) and local negotiations
- Service quality standards and customer satisfaction

This system change will destabilize labour-management relations on both sides of the table. Three core features of it will have the most impact on the industrial relations system — disaggregation of policy and service delivery; shifting transfer payments away from flat grants and towards performance-based funding; the introduction of a contract work system not only for sending work "out" but between service delivery units within the public service.

The movement to disaggregate the policy functions from service delivery — in effect unbundling and separating out service delivery

— will fundamentally destabilize the overall labour-management relations system. It will uncouple the existing representation system for both labour and management sides. Boundaries will be blurred. Who will be the employer? What will be the bargaining unit, and who is the bargaining agent? The impact of these changes will be felt most strongly at the levels of government which are currently involved in service delivery — provincial, regional and municipal.

St. Michael's Hospital, Toronto

By July, 1996, biochemistry, microbiology and haematology labs at St. Michael's hospital in Toronto had been rolled into a single core unit, with employees cross-trained in common functions. Reorganization is bringing smaller departments into larger ones, and will effect a twenty per cent reduction of St. Michael's 133 managers. Former food services, pharmacy and material handling departments, have been folded into a single department.

City of Peterborough

With city officials expecting a twenty-three per cent reduction in provincial transfers over three years, the province reduced transfers by thirty-six per cent in a single year. Peterborough's official unemployment rate is listed at twelve per cent, a figure the Social Planning Council puts at almost nineteen per cent. The provincial government reduced spending in the Peterborough area by $24.5 million. Cuts to the public and separate school boards totalled $9 million, Sir Sanford Fleming College lost $6.9 million, Trent University $3.5 million and area hospitals were reduced by $4.3 million.

Source: *Report on Business*, July 13, 1996

The transfer payments system is being altered, moving away from flat grants and transfers, towards conditional funding based on performance. In Ontario hospitals — the largest single centralized bargaining group in the country — local hospital budgets are now linked directly to productivity and performance with measurements taken between peer groups of hospitals. Performance comparisons introduce a form of competition into hospitals which will undermine centralized bargaining. Most hospital labour contracts are not negotiated, they are awarded by arbitrators on the basis of common criteria and patterns. In the future, if interest arbitrators conduct their business in the old way, they will simply wind up awarding layoffs.

Contracting out is an old and vexatious issue for labour-management relations. However, the coming public sector management model will usher in a pervasive system of contracting, not just "out" but within and between service delivery units in the public sector. This, in turn, introduces the concept of internal as well as external customers. Existing contract language devices which deal with contracting out will be marginalized in the new contractual context. What work belongs to whom and on what conditions will be fundamentally challenged. The leading test of this new contract environment will come in the municipalities.

Strikes and Contracting Out: OPSEU and GM, 1996

Contracting out and segregation of services is a trend begun in the private sector. The Alberta government's elimination of all its payroll processing is the same as General Motors walking away from its parts manufacturing.

OPSEU, Ontario's major provincial public service union, and the Ontario government had a much-publicized five-week strike in the spring of 1996. Like the GM-UAW situation discussed below, the core issue was employment security and contracting out — privatizing — work traditionally performed by OPSEU members.

The strike produced major gains for the government in new procedures to move work and people out, some new rights for individuals but little for the union. The example is worth exploring in some detail because it illustrates the difficulties of the present system. There is a myth that public servants have absolute job security or tenure. This is false. What they have are union contracts with such long and complicated rules for laying staff off that the time and costs involved have made layoffs virtually impossible. Also, the same rules apply to how jobs and work are defined and organized. The latter inhibit performance improvements, driving up costs and causing more layoffs. The result is the current vicious cycle for unions, management and employees.

The OPSEU Settlement

Under the contract won through the strike, if bargaining unit functions or jobs are transferred to the private sector, the government undertakes to make reasonable efforts to ensure that bargaining unit members are offered work with the new employer, with comparable terms and conditions of employment. Jobs will be offered on the basis of seniority. If the new wage is less than eighty-five per cent (85%) of current salary, workers can decline the transfer, receive a surplus notice and get enhanced severance (two weeks pay per year of service) plus existing rights to bumping, redeployment and retraining. Where divestment takes place through tendering, workers can submit a tender or bid.

The OPSEU agreement also provides for voluntary exit. If an OPSEU member leaves voluntarily, their job will be matched with a member on the surplus list. When the match is made, the surplus worker is assigned the position, subject to retraining if necessary. The employee taking the voluntary exit resigns and receives the enhanced severance of two weeks pay per year of service due all laid off workers.

The new rules for bumping by seniority provide that the employer must identify a bump within one week of giving layoff notice to an employee. If a junior employee in the same classification or in an employee's previous classification in the same ministry within a geographical area of forty kilometres, cannot be found, the employer must look province-wide in the same ministry, and finally in other ministries where the employee has previously worked, also within the forty kilometre radius. Three bumps are possible: an employee may dislocate a second employee, that second employee may do the same to a third.

Employees who cannot or choose not to bump another employee may be reassigned to a vacancy in their classification and ministry, within forty kilometres of their work location. If redeployment to a vacancy is not possible, the employee may be reassigned for retraining. Conditional on completing a retraining programme within a six-month period employees will be assigned to a vacancy in the same ministry and with the same or lower maximum salary, within the same geographical area.

Coincident with the OPSEU strike, the United Auto Workers (UAW) and General Motors (GM) were on strike in Ohio over the same general contracting out issues. From March 5 to March 22, 1996, UAW Local 696 conducted an eighteen-day strike against the Delphi Chassis Systems plant of GM. The parts shortage caused by the strike forced GM to close twenty-six of its twenty-nine North American plants and lay off more than 175,000 workers.

The UAW Settlement

The settlement reached in Ohio guarantees that no workers will be laid off and 417 new workers will be added to the Delphi plant over the next three years. In return for these job security guarantees, the union conceded to GM's demand for sub-contracting, or outsourcing, parts production when it increases the company's competitiveness to do so. In the union's view, prior to the strike GM was taking jobs away from the plants and sending work to small non-union shops in violation of local agreement contract language.

The job security language is set out in a commitment letter from GM. The Delphi Chassis plants will add 275 production employees immediately. Of these, 200 will ease overtime demands on the existing workforce, while the other seventy-five will provide ergonomic relief to various jobs throughout both plants. The remaining 142 workers will be skilled tradespeople and apprentices brought in over three years. The additions address numerous health and safety complaints lodged over the past year with regard to staffing levels and repetitive-motion injuries.

While GM will outsource some parts, the agreement calls for the company to provide the UAW with a list of upcoming product needs so that the plants can compete for this business. The company has the right to outsource, but the union has 150 days to respond and the chance to recapture the business.

Both strikes were major confrontations between large employers and large unions concerning contracting out. The UAW members kept and, in fact, increased their employment levels, while the OPSEU membership levels can only go down. Three lessons arise from these cases. First, the UAW result, at least in this case, sprung from its local strength. Most public sector unions are centrally strong and locally weak. Secondly, GM had core operations it wanted to retain. It is not clear what, if any, "core" operations the Harris government wishes to keep. Third, the union at UAW 696 plays a strategic role in information flow and potentially organizing alternate production strategies, while any parallel OPSEU role is simply missing. New contracts negotiated in September 1996, between the Canadian Auto Workers (CAW) and Chrysler in Canada and the UAW and Ford in the United States have followed this pattern.

Hard Bargaining in a New Environment

Change is happening in the public sector across Canada. It is a worldwide phenomenon as public organizations experiment with new management techniques like continuous improvement in service delivery, new technologies and contracting approaches, involvement of employee groups in consultation and work teams. International benchmarks for change are emerging and spawning a new vocabulary: managerialism, performance indicators, the Oregon Benchmarks, the Contractual State.

The combination of financial pressure and new organizational approaches is generating huge stress on the public sector industrial relations system. Something is going to give. Faced with a temporary crisis in the past over inflation-based wages and government deficits, wage controls were imposed on the system. The present challenge is greater and longer. It requires re-thinking the labour-management model itself. The last decade has seen major shifts in private sector labour-management relations. Work-teams, multi-skilling of employees and joint labour-management cooperation on industrial restructuring have become a commonplace. Ten years ago they were virtually unthinkable. Public sector labour and management are now faced with coming up with similar changes. But, in the public sector it is not just a matter of changing or transforming labour-management relationships. If a new deal is not worked out, there may simply a political exit by the government. GM fully intends to stay in the automobile business. Premiers like Ralph Klein in Alberta and Mike Harris in Ontario have no such base commitment to government services.

The direction and content of the turn in the public sector will not simply be a distributional spectator sport, watching to see whose ox gets gored. Nor will it be a matter of gaming the next move in the on-going labour-management chess match. The determinative issue will be the capacities of the public sector — individuals and organizations — to innovate. Can ways be found to supply needed health and community services in new ways, with lower costs and higher quality outcomes? How can more flexibility, productivity and mobility be brought to public sector labour markets? At the same time, these objectives can only be advanced with a committed and motivated workforce.

If these are the broad directions of change underway in the public sector, both in the narrow sense of government, and, more importantly, in the broad area of public services, the first public policy question raised is, "Is Wagnerism still in the public interest?" This demands an examination of the "labour issue" — the traditional view of public sector unions — and of public sector Wagnerism, the linchpin of public sector unionism (chapter 1). Beyond the traditional view, lies a discussion in greater depth of the development of New Public Management (NPM) in Canada and across OECD countries, as it impacts on organizational structures, service delivery, performance and quality measurement, the new operating environment of the public sector (chapter 2). How does this environment take shape in specific public sector areas? What does it mean in day-to-day, practical terms? Case histories of how the larger issues are playing out illustrate issues of particular relevance. A discussion of hospitals covers multi-skilling and performance-based budgeting. Material on municipalities focuses on contracting and performance measurement, and the case of Ontario Hydro offers room for discussion of privatization (chapters 3, 4 & 5). Reconciling the conflicting interests and expectation into new, "post-Wagnerist" directions for labour-management relations in the public sector will require a lot of hard bargaining (chapter 6).

— CHAPTER I —
A SYSTEM IN CRISIS

Public Sector Wagnerism
Public sector Wagnerism has been the dominant model for labour-management relations since unionism came to Canadian public employees in the 1960s and 1970s. The birthplace of Wagnerism was the American *New Deal National Labor Relations Act, 1936* also known as the *Wagner Act* for its sponsor, Senator Wagner of New York. At the heart of the *Wagner Act* industrial union model is job control unionism, a term for a system of job classifications, a wage rate structure and seniority-based work rules which reflect an adversarial relationship between labour and management in the workplace. The *Wagner Act*, in its original form, was directed to private sector mass production industries — such as steel and automobile manufacturing — largely male, permanent workforces engaged in standardized mass production with fixed, narrow job skills and rigid boundaries between the prerogatives of management and workers. The basic legal framework from *Wagner* was introduced in Canada by an order-in-council during World War II and passed into provincial labour laws in the later 1940s. This set the framework for an adversarial industrial relations system for Canadian private industries such as forestry, mining and manufacturing.

As they rapidly emerged in the 1960s and 1970s, Canadian public sector unions looked to the successful examples of the private sector unions such as the Steelworkers (United Steelworkers of America — USWA) and the Autoworkers (United Auto Workers — UAW, at the time) as benchmarks for what a "real union" should be. The fledging public sector unions drew many of their staff representatives and negotiators from the ranks of the industrial union staffs. A truncated version of the industrial union model thus came to be applied to public sector unions, with relatively little adaptation of union culture to the different economic, regulatory and operating environment in the public sector.

Stelco 1946 Contract, Nurses 1996 Hospital Contract

In 1946, the United Steelworkers of America negotiated their first formal labour contract with the Steel Company of Canada (Stelco). Along with the UAW-Ford contract in Windsor, this was one of the defining collective agreements framing the adversarial labour-management system for the postwar economy. That 1946 contract, laid beside a contemporary public sector contract — for instance, a 1996 hospital nurses' contract between an acute care hospital and the Ontario Nurses Association (ONA) — illustrates both the essential similarity of the contracts and the continued impact of the postwar private sector industrial relations model.

Collective Agreement Comparisons

Stelco '46	ONA '96
Management's Rights	
The Management of the plant and the direction of the working forces, including the right to direct, plan and control plant operations, to schedule working hours, and the right to hire, promote, demote, transfer, suspend or discharge employees for cause, or to release employees because of lack of work or for other legitimate reasons, or the right to introduce new and improved methods or facilities and to manage the plant in the traditional manner is vested exclusively in the Company, subject to the expressed provisions of this Agreement.	The Association recognizes that the management of the Hospital and the direction of working forces are fixed exclusively in the Hospital and shall remain solely with the Hospital, except as specifically limited by the provisions of this Agreement, and without restricting the generality of the foregoing, the Association acknowledges that it is the exclusive function of the Hospital to: maintain order, discipline and efficiency; hire, assign, retire, discharge, direct, promote, demote, classify, transfer, lay-off, recall and suspend or otherwise discipline nurses... determine all work procedures, the kind and location of equipment used, methods to be used, the allocation and number of nurses required from time to time, the services to be performed, standards of performance of all employees, work assignments, the hours of work and all other rights and responsibilities of management, not

	specifically modified elsewhere in this Agreement; establish, alter and enforce reasonable rules and regulations to be observed by the nurses. These rights shall not be exercised in a manner inconsistent with the provisions of this Agreement.

Seniority Rules

In all cases of promotion and in all cases of decrease or increase of working forces, the following factors shall be considered: a) Knowledge, efficiency and ability to perform the work. b) Physical fitness. c) Length of continuous service. Where factors a) and b) are relatively equal in the opinion of the Company, factor c) shall govern.	Nurses shall be selected for positions on the basis of their skill, ability and experience and qualifications. Where these factors are relatively equal amongst the nurses considered, seniority shall govern providing the successful applicant, if any, is qualified to perform the available work within an appropriate familiarization period.

Purpose of Collective Agreement

It is the intent and purpose of the parties hereto to set forth herein the basic Agreement covering wages, hours of work and conditions of employment to be observed between the parties hereto and to provide procedure for the prompt, equitable adjustment of alleged grievances to the end that there shall be no interruption or impeding of work, work stoppages, strikes or other interference with production during the life of this Agreement.	The general purpose of this agreement is to establish and maintain collective bargaining relations between the Hospital and the nurses covered by this agreement; to provide for ongoing means of communication between the Association and the Hospital and the prompt disposition of grievances and the final settlement of disputes and to establish and maintain mutually satisfactory salaries, hours of work and other conditions of employment in accordance with the provisions of this Agreement.

The similarity will come as no surprise to industrial relations practitioners, yet to an outside observer, the close family resemblance in the framework and content of these labour contracts would seem strange. These are two completely different kinds of organizations: a 1940s steel mill versus an acute care hospital fifty years later. These are different workforces: a traditionally low to semi-skilled manual and a professionally certified, university educated, white collar service. And the work itself is dramatically different: assembly-line type production of physical commodities versus customized, health care delivered to patients. However, the fundamental employment relationships, definitions and conditions are essentially the same. *By mutual consent of labour and management*, a 1940s private sector industrial relations model has been imposed on a 1990s public service delivery system. Such is the scope and power of public sector Wagnerism.

While the Wagner model was well-suited to the conditions of mass production industries in the 1930s and 1940s, this is not the case for the economic and organizational environment of the 1990s, in either the public or private sectors. Three central features of the Wagner industrial union model are problematic for the economic environment of the 1990s. And though this discussion relates to the pubic sector, the issues are no less true in the private. First, it has produced a multiplicity of fragmented, separate bargaining units even among employees with the same employer. Second, the legislative schema forces a radical separation of employer and employee interests, making cooperation difficult and as much a matter of law as attitude. Third, the system of job classifications and seniority-based work rules divide work into narrow and rigid categories, creating barriers for groupwork and expanded employee involvement in service delivery.

Crisis of the Wagner Act Model

- Fragmented bargaining units
- Radical separation of employer/employee interests
- Job structures and work rules

Fragmented Bargaining Units

The current system has fostered the proliferation of a multiplicity of fragmented bargaining units. The original Wagner model was based on one bargaining unit per industrial plant. In fact, often at employer urging, labour relations boards certified very narrow bargaining units, most often separating full-time and part-time employees, and office workers from production and maintenance workers. In the public sector, there are relatively more bargaining agents to deal with per site and the work rule and contractual provisions are often reinforced by the regulatory regime.

Radical fragmentation of bargaining units is a characteristic feature of the industrial relations landscape across the country. In the public sector this takes on an added twist. The timing of how and when certification rights were extended in the public sector, and traditions of white collar professionalism, meant that this general multiplicity of bargaining units was augmented by quasi-professional associations that emerged as different unions. Industrial unions have had long traditions of conflicts over the presence and bargaining objectives of their trades groups versus general production workers, but they were, at least for the most part, all in one union, be it USWA, CAW or Communications, Electrical and Paper Workers (CEP). However, in the public sector, these different occupational groups are typically represented by completely different and distinct groups, not only separate union locals but separate organizations altogether. For instance, within an Ontario hospital the general workforce will be represented by CUPE or the Service Employees International Union (SEIU), but the nurses have a separate organization, ONA, and the lab technicians belong to another organization (OPSEU). Similarly, school boards are split between different teachers unions' and non-teacher groups are represented by a variety of other unions.

In addition to creating duplication of organizational resources and bargaining requirements, this system has unique difficulties dealing effectively with workplace restructuring. Multi-skilling — where groups or teams of workers would rotate between assignments across traditional job classification boundaries — for instance, is difficult enough to negotiate with one union within one plant. Negotiating multi-skilling, work re-assignment as well as managing the employment impacts across these unrelated multi-union formations will be particularly difficult in broader public sector organizations because of the way the workforce is represented. In labour economics terminology, the broader public sector workforce and labour market are uniquely segmented. This labour market segmentation is reinforced by the system of trade union representation. Further, legislation such as the *Health Disciplines Acts 1982, 1994,* create additional regulatory barriers to adjustment of tasks, skills and workflow in service realignment within hospitals.

The present system has built up huge and unnecessary costs which will have to be reduced. However, it is a system ill-fitted to solving the cost problem. In a nut shell, it raises the spectre that once a new deal is devised, how and with whom do you negotiate it? Should it be embodied in labour contracts or in the legislation and regulations?

Employer-Employee Interests

The second dysfunctional feature of the *Wagner Act* model is the radical separation of employer and employee interests. The system of mass production in the classic industries like steel and auto was well-served in the 1940s and 1950s by the rigid separation of the union mandated to negotiate wages, benefits and working conditions, but uninvolved in management of the plant. Walter Reuther of the UAW tried to negotiate production, investment and product issues in 1948 with General Motors, but his innovative proposals were rejected. In private industry, as the new norms of production, arising in particular from the Japanese auto industry, change with new technology and communications developments, employee involvement and empowerment proposals, drastic reductions in levels of supervision, coupled with new expectations and skills for line workers are transforming the workplace. In unionized sites, these new directions in work organization and human resource management wrestle with the traditions, norms and contract provisions inherited from the Wagner era. These are lively and contentious issues within the private sector for unions such as the Canadian Auto Workers, United Steel Workers of America, Communications, Electrical and Paper Workers and United Food and Commercial Workers (UFCW). (Kumar 1995)

The Wagner legislation did not directly create the management's rights provisions that dominate postwar collective agreements. But, the normative framework embedded in the Act created the ground rules for its emergence, for instance, in the 1942 contract between GM and the UAW. However, faced with a dramatic need to change, as the example of Algoma Steel illustrates, the parties can produce new tradeoffs and new relationships on the shopfloor. At Algoma Steel in Sault Ste. Marie, Ontario, the traditional management's rights clause has been eliminated to accommodate the role taken by shopfloor joint committees and individual employees in the co-management of production scheduling, technology, quality and departmental budgeting. Similar innovations have been occurring in the private sector following a decade of much controversy between labour and management, and within and between unions facing dramatic transformation in the international economy. The public sector, which has not even begun this discussion in a broad way, will not have a decade to work it out. Fiscal pressures will drive change much more quickly than that. Not all public sector managers will react to the changes by attempting to re-align employer and employee interests in new ways. Some will be tempted to re-assert traditional managements rights more aggressively and unilaterally. This will ultimately fail.

A New Understanding of Public Sector Employment Relations

The theory and practice of public sector industrial relations have, to date, been articulated in terms of a core factor of political constraint. Traditional analyses of public sector unionism have focused on the government's role as employer and legislator, public sector unionization rates, strikes and pay levels. While these issues are not unimportant or misplaced, recently they have been overtaken by government fiscal problems, new contracting arrangements, disaggregation of public service delivery, and productivity and performance measurement. The system is now confronted with a qualitatively different factor: fundamental economic constraint. Union activists are still inclined to interpret this sea change as a political, rather than economic, imperative. And, most decision-makers in the public sector, as well as arbitrators and commentators, still perceive public sector labour-management dynamics in the old terms.

A recent major collection of essays on Canadian public sector collective bargaining — Gene Swimmer and Mark Thompson's *Public Sector Collective Bargaining in Canada* — begins from the perspective that the defining characteristic of bargaining in the public sector is that it is an exercise in political, not economic, power. In this analysis, the public employer's primary concern is public opinion and the concomitant prospect of re-election, rather than long-term profit maximization. The public sector strike is construed as a political weapon and public reaction is the pressure forcing the employer to settle.

Swimmer and Thompson raise concerns about the prospect of a future in which governments do not respect the terms of collective agreements:

> If government as legislator overrides the procedures and standards negotiated previously by government as employer, what is left for negotiations and the other practices of public sector industrial relations? (Swimmer and Thompson, 1995)

This leads them to conjecture a future public sector with a highly organized work force employed under conditions established unilaterally by the employer. They forsee five possible futures, all of which assume a fundamental political driver of public sector industrial relations:

- Back to the Past — a return to the features of the association-consultation model where employees would be highly organized but their representatives would have little or no bargaining power.
- Struggle in the Streets — coordination of bargaining strategy by major unions with centralized bargaining structures, relatively public negotiations and impasses resolved by special legislation.
- A Sullen Truce — governments restrict compensation and collective bargaining for periods of time during which unions seek to lobby support to change policies.

- A New Golden Age — a return to the free collective bargaining of the 1960s and 1970s facilitated by recovery in government revenues and in public expectations of government services.
- Power-Sharing — governments faced with restraints seek to negotiate with unions on the terms of how to reallocate spending with the objective of reaching a new productivity bargain.

If government as legislator overrides the procedures and standards negotiated previously by government as employer, what is left for negotiations and the other practices of public sector industrial relations? This is the traditional concern about public sector industrial relations. But history may have overtaken this view.

What if the dynamics turn on another factor, the fact that, for the overwhelming majority of public sector employees, *the central government is not the employer*? Direct employees of federal and provincial governments are less than fifteen per cent (15%) of the total public sector. Eighty-five per cent (85%) are in the broader public sector (BPS), employed by individual hospitals, school boards, municipalities, social and other agencies. The recent experience of Alberta and the "success" of the Klein government's programme suggests another option — the neo-voluntarist one — that may become more prevalent across the system.

In this scenario, bargaining occurs at some distance from those politically responsible for funding reductions. The pervasive transfer payment system between levels of government, and even more importantly, between central governments and local transfer agencies, allows a central government — like the Alberta provincial government — to cut transfers, then let the local parties sort out the consequences of reduced financing. On the surface, collective bargaining and union rights are preserved. Local management is left free to manage and the political level does not participate, let alone own, the process.

The major area in which the new economics of public sector collective bargaining will play itself out is not in the direct forum of government as employer, but in the broad public sector where most public sector workers are employed and where local management is the employer. The dynamics here will be different from those where political constraint dominated.

Public Sector Unions on Work Organization and Multi-Skilling

Public sector job control unionism has set up a particular dynamic for workplace change that does and does not match the pattern of private sector industrial relations. Public sector emphasis on job security has reinforced an emphasis on seniority-based work rules and narrow job classifications. In addition, public sector bargaining agents have linked job security issues to public policy and political lobbying issues. While public sector union bodies have started sending signals that they are prepared to bargain new approaches, these signals are heavily qualified by attachments to the old system of job control unionism.

In fact, the public and private sectors have been moving in opposite directions in recent years. While the public sector has moved toward increasingly rigid rules and proliferation of job titles, the private sector — at different speeds and with variations across industries — has been adopting work teams, multi-skilling and more flexibility.

Trends in Job Structures & Work Rules

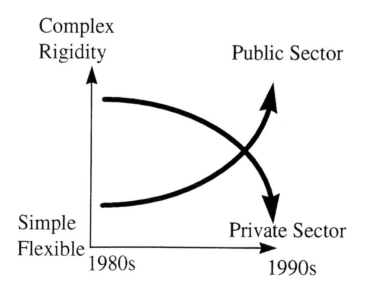

The overall perspective of public sector union leaders on workplace reform and labour-management cooperation is well-summarized in the words of James Clancy, national president of the National Union of Public and General Employees (NUPGE).

> Can we say that workers have gained more control at the end of the exercise or less control? We have got to answer that question. And, is the union's role and authority enhanced or diminished? Those are the two fundamental questions that we have to always put up as the litmus test for any involvement in the "re-design" of government. (NUPGE 1994)

NUPGE has articulated explicit preconditions for union participation in the public sector reform process:
- The process cannot be defined by a pre-determined agenda of management.
- It must lead to worker empowerment.
- The union must have equal standing with management.
- It must have support and involvement of the membership at all levels.
- It must have a written commitment to employment security.
- It must take place within a collective bargaining framework and not be a substitute for collective bargaining.
- It must take place in a pro-public sector environment.
- There must be a moratorium on public sector bashing.
- The union must have a say on the use of any cost savings achieved as the result of the process.
- There must be full and open disclosure of information from management. (NUPGE 1994)

These are all concerns that a union understandably has about representing its members. However, this list resembles a political campaign strategy more than a bargaining programme. It is unlikely that the current fiscal environment will allow for such political nuances. But, NUPGE is a federation of affiliated unions, not a direct bargaining agent itself.

The Canadian Union of Public Employees is the largest union in the country and has developed an explicit bargaining strategy around the issues of new management techniques and workplace restructuring. In CUPE's view, correctly, the restructuring of the 1990s is a double-edged sword. It can be constructive and lead to improved services, or it can take the form of funding, staff and service cutbacks. CUPE argues that the current rhetoric of reform — downsizing, productivity pressures, TQM, concessions, layoffs — is being used to justify and obscure the harsh reality of cuts in jobs and services. The union believes that some services need to be reformed, but reforms should be based on principles that ensure community needs are met, that public employees are treated fairly, and that services will remain reliable, equitable and accessible. (CUPE 1994)

CUPE has published *Twelve Principles for Public Sector Reform,* as follows:

1. Public services must be adequately funded.
2. Not-for-profit public sector delivery of public services ensures that all available resources are directed to the provision of services.
3. Clear standards must be established and retained for the delivery of public services.
4. Services must be easily and fully accessible.
5. Services must be comprehensive.
6. Health and safety must be preserved.
7. Workers affected by restructuring must have access to appropriate adjustment and training programs.
8. Skills training and retraining must be an essential part of adjustment strategies.
9. Existing agreements may need to be strengthened.
10. The union must be consulted and have a say in all restructuring programs and in decisions affecting public sector delivery.
11. Management and labour share responsibilities for maintaining quality services.
12. CUPE should, wherever possible, work closely with its non-labour allies. (CUPE 1994)

The CUPE principles are heavily tilted towards participative process and social policy issues. In the 1980s, public sector unions greatly expanded their roles as social policy advocacy groups. In the 1990s, their mettle will be tested as bargaining agents. The key question is *What role will the union assume as a bargaining agent in the local labour-management relationships and workplaces where it directly represents its members with the employer?* There are instances where the union has applied the above principles successfully in local worksites. One is the Quebec City municipal agreement with CUPE Local 1638, in which the collective agreement states that the parties agree to "collaborate in evaluating any measure capable of improving the quality of services."

As the foregoing lists indicate, development of strategic perspectives on a new productivity deal in the public sector has started on the union side. Thus far, there has been significantly less development from management, at least in public. Mutually beneficial productivity bargaining can allow for improvements in wages and working conditions. For instance, it has been suggested that unions could bargain over the development of completely autonomous working arrangements at the individual or small workgroup level.

Why Are Things So Rigid?

The rigidity of labour contract job classifications, work rules and union resistance to change are economically rational. The Wagner system was a direct outgrowth of the Great Depression and massive unemployment. In a market-based economy, workers' only source of employment security is legal protection within the workplace. Tight rules mean protection against arbitrary decisions by supervisors and easy dismissal by employers. On the management side, in a growth period, this was an acceptable price to pay for labour peace and predictable costs.

The end of the growth period and a new era of mass layoffs have suddenly arrived in the public sector. The estimated costs to a worker being permanently laid off is about equivalent to the loss of a $100,000 investment destroyed in a disaster. It is not surprising that unions fight hard. Less acknowledged are the costs to the employer. The involuntary dismissal of a unionized employee brings a total cost of about $40,000 to the employer. To hire and train a new person costs anywhere from $7,000 to $40,000.

The paradox is that Wagnerism's rigid contracts worked well for both parties in the past. Unionized workers had much better job security than on the open market, and often had above average wages. Employers had labour stability and predictability in the growth stage. However, in times of economic trouble, the contracts only allow for layoffs, not alternate work arrangements like job sharing, multi-skilling or part-time work. This results in huge costs for workers, and further costs for employers. Both parties are stuck, with no options within the current system.

It is probably inherent to the traditions, institutional framework and psychology of the situation that the unions' position on public sector restructuring will be a response to the initiatives of the employer. The whole postwar framework of Wagnerism was premised on the employer's right of initiative and union response. Control of all significant decisions about change in the workplace — new technology, size and allocation of the workforce, determination of the content and flow of production and products — were management's prerogative. The first steps to the future will be the emerging new managerialism among public sector employers and governments, because it is the employers who have the initiative and momentum in the current situation.

An American Perspective: The Clinton Administration, Re-inventing Government and Public Sector Labour-Management Relations Reform

The Clinton administration is publicly commited to a general policy of consensus in labour-management relations. To explore private sector issues, the administration established The Commission on the Future of Worker-Management. For the public sector, The National Partnership Council brings public sector managers and federal unions together to help streamline and improve the effectiveness of federal government operations.

In 1994, Robert Reich's Task Force on Excellence in State and Local Government through Labour Management Cooperation was established to investigate the current state of labour-management cooperation. It is empowered to look at legal frameworks, improve workplace dispute resolution processes and inter-governmental coordination.

The premise for these initiatives is that employees know more about their jobs than anyone else. High-performance public sector workplaces depend on three key principles:
- citizen satisfaction
- continuous and long-term improvement in work processes and products
- the total involvement of employees and their unions in the process of change.

Similarly, the AFL-CIO takes the position that collective bargaining is an inclusive process, incorporating *all aspects* of the relationship between management and its employees and their union. This cooperative relationship does not replace collective bargaining; it is a vital part of the total collective bargaining process according to the AFL-CIO. They believe that successful labour-management partnerships require:
- employment security
- the recognition of the union as a full and equal partner
- open communication
- the delegation of authority and sharing of power
- commitment, training, patience, and faith.

The barriers to successful labour-management partnership which must be overcome are:
- resistant leadership
- cumbersome personnel and bureaucratic systems
- inadequate budgets
- a lack of commitment to skills upgrading
- the need for consolidation and coordination of programs and services
- outdated technology.

AFL-CIO publications stress that the continued denial of collective bargaining rights to nearly six million state and local government employees remains a serious obstacle to reform.

In the U.S., as indicated, the administration and the central labour federation have convergent views about parallel changes in public administration and labour relations. However, at the state and local levels, most workers lack legal collective bargaining rights. In Canada, virtually every public employee has been eligible for unionization and has a labour contract. Modification in Canada requires a wholesale change in our overall concept of public sector labour-management relations.

The Traditional Concept of Public Sector and Private Sector Differences

The performance of the public sector industrial relations system is frequently viewed and judged by policymakers, the public at large and, to some extent, academic commentators in terms of wages and strikes in the public and private sector.

The political nature of the employer — that government, responsible to the people through elections, is the employer — has been taken as the central, *generic* principle of public sector industrial relations. Existing public sector industrial relations research stresses the importance of the government, as an employer of labour, being a political entity. Therefore, political rather than economic influences are central in public sector industrial relations. However, a review of the 1980s suggests that the state's role as a macroeconomic regulator, rather than as an employer of labour, has been paramount in shaping public sector industrial relations.

Public Sector Union Growth and Density

As stated, the public sector is the most highly unionized segment of the economy. The following graphic gives rates of union density for major industries across Canada. Union density is expressed as the percentage of employees in the industry covered by collective agreements.

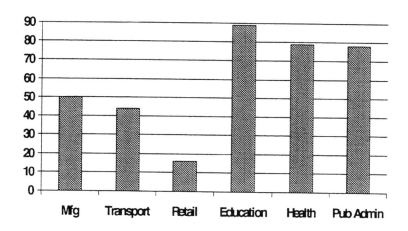

Public Sector Union Density
(% of employees covered by collective agreements, 1984)

(Rose 1995)

Over the last twenty years growth rates of public sector unions have been roughly double those of the private sector. Between 1981 and 1992, the net estimated gain of 720,116 public sector members exceeds the total increase in Canadian union membership of 692,279 during the period. Thus, net union growth for the period occurred almost exclusively in the public sector.

Observers comment that the three major public sector unions — CUPE, NUPGE and the Public Service Alliance of Canada (PSAC) — resulted from mergers which weakened central authority and created a lack of experienced leadership. Furthermore, large elements of their membership lacked experience in militant action in either bargaining or political arenas. The conventional wisdom was that these organizations grew under relatively benign conditions and were not well equipped to cope with adversity. As a result, public sector unions became adept at centrally-managed social policy advocacy and political campaigns, but much less effective at centrally-coordinated or local bargaining programs. For evidence of this phenomenon, we need look no further than the modest results of the 1996 OPSEU strike and relative acquiesence in local bargaining in the face of the twenty per cent (20%) cutbacks by the Alberta and Ontario governments.

Public Sector Compensation

Are public employees paid more than private employees in comparable jobs and with comparable skills? Most studies show that public sector wages, particularly benefits, have a "premium" — that is are higher than — their private counterparts at the lower-income and skill levels. The formers' salaries lag behind the latters' at the professional and senior management levels. The most meaningful comparison most people make is between relative wage increases — are they falling behind? Broad comparisons show that many public groups have had rates of increase above their private counterparts over the course of the last decade.

Public and Private Cumulative Wage Increases 1978-92 (1978 Base = 100)

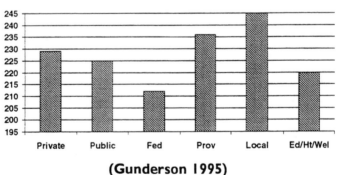

(Gunderson 1995)

Theory suggests that there is at least a *potential* for an upward bias to public sector wages, because the only constraint is political will, rather than market competition. In addition, because the true costs of employee benefits can be put off or spread over a period of time, it is argued that politicians will be particularly vulnerable to conceding overly generous benefits. Thus, it is imperative that both wages and non-wage outcomes be looked at.

The most recent studies (Gunderson & Reid, 1995) indicate that a public sector wage advantage does exist, although it is not large, in the neighbourhood of five to ten per cent (5-10%). The advantage is larger at the provincial and local as opposed to the federal level, greater for females as opposed to males, and for low-waged workers as opposed to high-wage workers. Low-waged women working in provincial and municipal governments, schools and hospitals, have gained the most from public sector unionization.

The public sector wage advancement appears to be declining, especially for males, although it seems to be increasing for females. Settlements tend to be volatile, sometimes unusually high and temporary, often reflecting a "catch-up" to earlier private sector agreements. They then tend to dissipate over time. Over the long run, wage settlements in the public and private sectors tend to be fairly similar.

Although evidence is limited, fringe benefits are likely to be greater in the public rather than the private sector, increasing rather than offsetting the slight wage premium.

The impact of unions on wages is smaller in the public sector than in the private — the spread between union and non-union wages is greater in the private sector — though arbitration imparts a slight upward bias to wage settlements in the public sector. It should be emphasized, however, that the Canadian evidence is based on only a small number of studies, most of which do not deal with the important period of the 1980s and 1990s.

The public-private sector wage differential has changed considerably in the last thirty years, from a disadvantage, in the 1950s, to an advantage in the 1960s and 1970s. This corresponds to the increase in unionization over that period, suggesting that much of the public sector gain may reflect a union wage effect, given the high degree of unionization in the public sector.

Public Sector Strikes

While strike activity is declining markedly in the private sector, this is not so in the public, which accounts for an increasing share of overall strike action. The number of days lost due to strikes has varied considerably since the mid-1970s, with a slight downward trend in the private sector and a relatively steady level in the public. As a result, public sector strike action has accounted for a larger proportion of the total, showing a rise from an average of just under twenty per cent (20%) of total strike activity in the mid-1970s to over thirty per cent (30%) in 1991. There is considerable annual variability; the public sector "share" has ranged from a low of ten per cent (10%) in 1986 to a high of fifty per cent (50%) in 1983 and 1991.

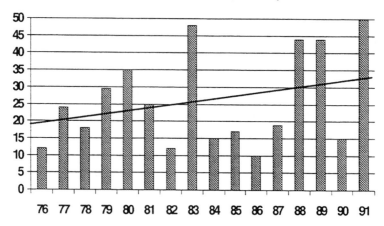

Public Sector Strikes 1976-91
(% of Total Strike Days Lost)

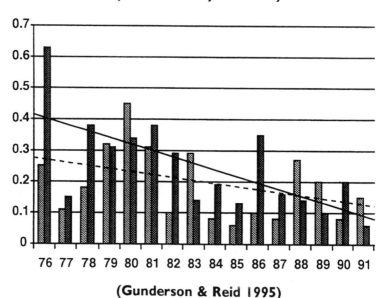

Public & Private Sector Strikes 1976-91
(% of Total Days Worked)

(Gunderson & Reid 1995)

The decline in private sector strike activity is considerably more pronounced when expressed as a percentage of days worked, since employment and days worked have increased since the mid-1970s. In contrast, the public sector decline was much lower. By 1988 the trend in the number of public sector days lost as a percentage of days worked exceeded that of the private sector.

Striking in the public sector varies by different components of the sector. A few large key strikes can dominate the picture in any one year. In fact, strikes are less common in the public sector than in the private; disputes — defined as arbitrations, strikes or legislated settlements — are more common in the public domain, although they are declining over time. The number of strikes is decreasing in both the private and public sectors, with days lost due to strikes declining in the private sector and roughly constant in the public. Overall, while most measures of strike activity show signs of abatement in the private sector, this is much less so in the public.

However, in the public sector, the potential effect of strikes is more severe. There are few good substitutes for what are often essential services or outputs. The consumers of public services cannot always go elsewhere when a service is not provided. In fact, they continue to pay tax revenues for services *they do not receive.* The cost to the employer is typically the political cost of disgruntled voters, rather than the economic cost of lost revenues. Though the strikers lose wages, the employer often continues to receive revenues. Loss of "market share" is seldom a factor. No tax rebates are offered to taxpayers who "pay for" but do not receive public services interrupted because of a strike. As a result, the economic dynamics of public sector strikes are different. In the private sector, strikes are economic trials of lost profit versus lost wages. In the public arena, employers "make" money during strikes, while employees lose wages and the public loses services.

Public Sector Arbitration

Notwithstanding the regular use of the language of "free collective bargaining" in the public sector, the majority of public sector employees, from hospital employees to doctors, largely function under a system of administered, or arbitrated, wage and salary setting. Most public sector wage determination does not result from either markets or the bargaining process. The province of Saskatchewan is the only Canadian jurisdiction where free collective bargaining for wages is the norm. There, public employees across the board are under the same labour relations legislation as those in the private. In all other Canadian jurisdictions, special labour relations statutes or alternate wage-determination mechanisms, typically providing for arbitration of disputes apply to the public sector.

The system of public sector wage arbitration — also known as interest arbitration — has been the subject of academic study. These studies have concluded that the system is flawed in two key respects: that unionized public sector groups are only compared with each other, and the system has generated a consistent upward wage bias, consistently increasing wages regardless of what is happening in the rest of the economy. (Hebdon, 1996)

When public sector unionization was introduced in the mid-1960s, interest arbitration was also introduced, in exchange for limitations on the right of essential service employees to strike. The early arbitrators, when faced with defining the parameters for public sector wage awards, followed a leading Ontario case from 1966, in which arbitrator Harry Arthurs defined the essential constraint on pay raises as the "employer's ability to pay." This created a real constraint, ultimately related to the transfer system of funding, to the upward movement of broader public sector employees' wages. Government funding put an absolute limit on wages. For the first decade of public sector unionization this system worked, but it could not cope with the inflation environment of the mid-1970s. Public sector wages seriously lagged inflation adjustments, particularly compared to private sector unionized contracts, which more often had cost of living allowance (COLA) provisions. In the period 1974-76, the system broke down in a series of wild cat strikes, and the jailing of public sector union leaders such as CUPE President Grace Hartman and Sean O'Flynn of OPSEU. The result was a discrediting of interest arbitration.

The interest arbitration system regained some legitimacy in the late 1970s, at least with employee groups, when a number of influential Canadian arbitrators, such as Howard Brown, broke with tradition and rejected the criterion of employer ability to pay. To be clear, this did not mean that arbitrators believed there were no economic limits. Instead, it meant that arbitrators could look further afield than government funding levels to judge what fair wages would be. They relied on economic criteria including inflation, broad productivity trends and wage comparability. From the early 1980s, wage arbitration consolidated around these general economic indicators as a basis for wage determination in the broader public sector. This stabilized the system through the 1980s, in which, overall, there was substantial growth in public spending, in spite of the movements in the business cycle. For example, public sector wage increases continued throughout the major recessions of 1981-83 and 1990-91, despite the decline in the overall economy.

The result was foreseeable, though perhaps not immediately evident. Reliance on general macroeconomic indicators such as inflation measured through the consumer price index (CPI) and general trends in productivity and income growth when combined with wage and occupational relativity comparisons, have an inherent upward bias. Given our growing population and some inflation, without a dramatic recession or depression, these indicators combined will virtually always have an upward direction, that is, cause a rise in wages.

For a time this problem was not directly evident. Government revenues continued to grow, even during the downturn of the early 1980s. Public sector wages at the time were overcoming much of the 1970s inflation-lag. The problem developed through cumulative effect. By the end of the 1980s, public sector wage patterns were consistently surpassing the private sector in relative and absolute terms. As well, by the early 1990s public sector wage patterns were seriously outstripping the path of government revenues which, particularly at the provincial level went flat or into decline. Ontario, which suffered the deepest economic decline during the post free trade recession in 1991 and 1992, witnessed an actual fall in revenues for the first time since the depression of the 1930s.

The problem is not inherent to arbitrators. Arbitration could be improved by standing panels of arbitrators for each sector or subsector, which in turn could reduce the randomness and leapfrogging that traditionally occurs as one arbitration outcome is used to leverage the next. More fundamentally, what is required is a change in what comes before arbitrators. A shift is needed in the fiscal environment for broader public sector operations. Economic performance needs to play a much more important role, and has the potential for presenting arbitrators with a different set of signals, allowing then to do their job in light of real tradeoffs over wages, productivity and employment outcomes. If the arbitration system simply attempts to resume business as usual in the future, in reality the outcome will be arbitrators awarding not wage increases but layoffs, because of government budgets and declining operating grants. Awarding wage increases which are not offset by productivity or efficiency gains will result in reduced employment. Where transfers are based on relative performance, awarding standardized increases without considering local performance will also result in layoffs.

The objective of the arbitration system was to provide for increases in earnings in return for standardized labour inputs and labour peace. Ironically, its degree of success over the years is a major source of resistance to serious change for both labour and management. Ability to pay will return to the negotiating table and arbitration hearings. But, this time the issues will be framed as unit costs of service and relative performance of local organizations compared to their peers. It will not be based on simple levels of block transfers from central government.

The Ghost in Public Sector Bargaining

It is in Quebec, to date, that the issue of the government role in public sector negotiations and indeed the politicization of labour-management negotiations has been played out most dramatically. The outcome of over two decades of the process has left commentators with very sobering conclusions about the prospects for change. In a nutshell, centralized bargaining has been good for cranking wages up, and occasionally for shrinking them. It is not good for dealing with costs and quality of services.

In the early 1960s, the Confederation of National Trade Unions (CNTU) always asked in its local or regional negotiations that the ghost — the government — come out of the closet. During that period, local Quebec management could not make decisions on monetary matters without central government approval. In the 1966 round, the government sat down at the table. The union had what it wanted, more bargaining power through the sheer size and the importance of the services involved. It also had what it did not want — opposing negotiators who were well-organized and much more powerful than the previous local hospital representatives.

Thirty years later the question remains: is true bargaining possible between a provincial government, laden with tight financial constraints and a huge union structure? The last ten years suggests the answer is no, or close to no. For the government, the theory of state sovereignty, the basis of the parliamentary system, places limits on the total aggregate compensation available. There is some question whether government wage policy can be bargainable. At the same time that elected governments have large commitments where they have to allocate limited public revenues, public employees have a right to fair treatment and wages. Public sector unions, however, have demonstrated very limited ability to be truly co-responsible for adverse decisions such as limiting or eliminating services or jobs, combining bargianing units or radically re-organizing work. For all these reasons, centralized solutions are likely to be the exceptions more than the rule in the next decade of public sector collective bargaining.

Decentralization can take many forms. But, it can work only if certain basic rules are established and strictly adhered to. For instance, complete local bargaining responsibility would be possible if every hospital or other government institution received a certain budget, and was free to use it for its clients in their best interest, according to its own judgment. The budget could never be changed except in dramatic circumstances; otherwise the bargaining would move rapidly from the local to a higher, perhaps the highest, level.

If — and this is a big if — all monetary questions were removed from bargaining, local decentralized negotiations would develop where management and employees wanted to cooperate.

In any political context with economic restrictions, it is hard to imagine union representatives making true and important concessions. It is so much easier to keep answering "no" and leave the social burden to the government, which will then have to legislate. Essentially this has been the history of public sector bargaining in Quebec.

Business Process Re-engineering and Wagnerism

Close at hand, the interface between Wagnerism and public sector "restructuring" is confronting management-initiated change in the form of Business Process Re-engineering (BPR). Since 1990, Business Process Re-engineering has become widely popular in management circles as a change strategy when small incremental improvement in the way an organization operates is too little or too late. It is not surprising that, in the face of massive budget cuts and draconian policy changes, public sector managers are resorting to BPR as a ready solution to their problems. Unfortunately, BPR itself is also in trouble.

The problems with BPR implementation are similar in the public and private sectors. In fact, Pacific Bell's experience with BPR is not unlike what is about to happen in the Canadian public sector. Pacific Bell is seventy per cent (70%) unionized and has large legacy operations and computer systems, not unlike a hospital, school board or large municipality.

The promise of BPR is large scale rapid change, with dazzling outcomes: seventy-five to eighty per cent (75-80%) reductions in costs, fifty per cent plus (50%+) improvements in cycle times, ninety-five to one hundred per cent (95-100%) customer satisfaction. Longitudinal studies show that the actual achievements are much more modest: fifty per cent (50%) of the cost targets, twice as long to implement. The issues go to the heart of the BPR approach.

- Re-engineering design may be radical, but implementation is incremental.
- Re-engineering design assumes clean slate change. However, implementation will be limited by those constraints that management cannot or will not remove.

- Re-engineering design focuses on end-to-end process re-design. Re-engineering implementation often focuses on the perceived most broken pieces.
- Re-engineering design is top-down directed, but implementation requires acceptance bottom-up.
- Re-engineering design is enabled by information technology, but the implementation is often initiated without much of the assumed information technology capability.

So how is Business Process Re-engineering likely to play in the public sector? To date it has barely dealt with labour-management relations. For the most part, it is being addressed in small scale department-level experiments, hidden away from union head offices and avoidance of the collective agreement. The top down change assumption in BPR will flounder in dealing with both labour and management. Bottom up buy-in will necessarily require union sanction and participation. That is why union positions on work re-organization and re-skilling are critical. For management, the effect of decentralization of authority into business units is that a central corporate office, let alone its human resources professionals, is less and less able to centrally sanction the implementation of specific change processes. Decentralization in heavily dependent on buy-in by departmental and line supervision. The second major problem is that most ambitious BPR designs require major new investments in information technology. At a time when operating budgets are being massively rolled back, there is no funding for major new information technology investments. Therefore, BPR designs underperform.

The downward spiral for BPR brings us back to the labour-management issue. Limits on central mandating of change means that organizations will regress towards incrementalism, one department or business unit at a time. In the absence of major new information technology, change is even more dependent on human resource factors like collocation of employees and multi-tasking/multi-skilling. Major changes in the latter require dramatic transformation in the collective agreements and work rules. In both cases what is needed is strategic, negotiated restructuring. Few local managements have a developed strategy for negotiated restructuring. Neither do they trust their own central organizations of hospital, municipal or school board associations to negotiate restructuring. On the central union side, development of policies for strategic restructuring negotiations are underdeveloped, and their local leadership has not been educated to carry the ball on their own.

The current situation is a confusing stalemate. Central solutions have only limited value. Real answers will be found locally. However, the finding of those answers will have to await the BPR re-engineers spinning out their wheels.

The Beginning of the End or the End of the Beginning?

In *Public Sector Collective Bargaining in Canada* editors Swimmer and Thompson raise the challenging question of whether the 1990s mark "The beginning of the end or the end of the beginning?" It is possible to say that real collective bargaining is about to begin in the public sector, and the privileged period of the "industrial" or Wagner model has come to an end.

— CHAPTER 2 —
THE NEW MANAGERIALISM

Current changes in the public sector are not merely a rotation from centrist or left-centre politics to right-wing dogma. While there is no doubt that, at times, political ideology plays an important role in the direction, extent and timing of change, the pressure for change should not be dismissed as simply the implementation of an ideological or corporate agenda. By missing this point, labour leaders and activists can misread important potential opportunities and, in extreme cases, bargain themselves into a "no-exit" corner. Beyond politics are the underlying drivers pushing transformation in the public sector. New attitudes, new technologies and fiscal pressures have forced private sector management to do more with less, which has resulted in opening new directions in labour-management relations. The same factors apply in the public sector. This new environment has given rise to the new public sector managerialism and consequent pressure for a transformation of public sector labour-management relations.

The Drivers of Change

Information Technologies (IT)

New information technologies, which enable services to be delivered in new ways may, in fact, facilitate what some politicians want to do anyway. The availability of payroll servicing companies and rapid computerized communications technology has allowed the Alberta government to contract out all of its payroll processing, a move that fits well with the Klein government's philosophy of smaller government. This invites some public sector managers to conjure up images of "virtual" hospitals and municipalities. All generic functions within government, such as payroll data processing, accounting and purchasing, may be vulnerable to contracting out. Similarly, in hospitals, dietary, laundry, laboratories and supplies may be equally vulnerable, not to computerization per se, but to high speed computer-coordinated services delivered from outside.

New Service Delivery Models

IT also makes possible new service delivery models to clients and the public. For example, direct bank deposit combined with phone and resume writing facilities for employable welfare recipients means that social workers can spend more time in pro-active assistance to people seeking work and less time processing cheques and filing forms. Technologically, there is no need for anyone to ever line up for a standard automobile or driver license renewal.

Fiscal Constraints

There is a serious gap between government revenues and expenditure. Our policy commitment to public services cannot be matched by resources and costs. Our tax system could be fairer and more effective but the problem cannot be taxed away. Canadians have borne the brunt of major income tax increases, as well as consumption taxes, but their sacrifices have been gobbled up by deficits and debt-servicing. There is no solution to this problem without significantly improving on the quality and unit costs of services in the public sector. The economics of public finance have changed permanently, and as definitively as the Atlantic fish stocks.

New Public Management Globally

The broad directions and developments in the New Public Management (NPM) were the subject of a recent study by the Organization for Economic Cooperation and Development (OECD), the inter-government organization of the most industrialized countries. The study found a common core of measures being introduced across a wide number of countries with a range of conservative, liberal and social-democratic governments. According to OECD work, the common core of New Public Management comprises:

- Cost cutting and greater accountability
- Disaggregating bureaucracies into separate agencies
- Decentralization of management authority

- Purchase-Provider service split
- Performance targets, indicators and output objectives
- Use of market and quasi-market mechanisms
- Decreased job tenure, decreased standard benefits
- Employment contracts, pay by performance, local conditions
- Service quality standards and customer standards

Of these, it is particularly the purchaser-provider split, disaggregating bureaucracies into separate agencies, and the introduction of market and quasi-market mechanisms that will have the greatest impact on labour-management relations.

The OECD study indicates that these are general trends across the public sector in all the advanced technology economies for managing the public sector and public services and go beyond local politics.

The Roots of Change

Present changes in the philosophy of government are rooted in Margaret Thatcher's Conservative government in Britain and the 1983-84 Labour government in New Zealand, political developments more than a decade ago.

From traditional public administration, focused on central administrators and hierarchical bureaucracy, there has been a structural shift to local management and the use of market and market-type mechanisms. The Thatcher and the New Zealand Labour governments undertook an immediate and radical move away from government departments and centralized service delivery towards rapid privatization. In the British National Health Service (NHS) Thatcher established that the government would purchase services from local physicians in groups and new "trust" hospitals, rather than have direct government administration of local service delivery. This is, in essence, the genesis of the public sector purchaser-provider split. In the New Zealand case, this split was generalized into a new theory — the Contract State — where virtually all services would be delivered under contract whether internally, between government departments or externally, by private or external public contractors.

The direction of change is illustrated in the following graphic, where UK1 corresponds to the Thatcher government in Britain and UK2 is the later, John Major, government. NZ1 refers to the Labour government in New Zealand and NZ2 is the New Zealand National government. The acronym MTM at the bottom of the chart stands for market type mechanisms. The initial dramatic shift in the traditional public sector structure in both countries is illustrated by the move from the top left quadrant, down and to the right, away from the bureaucracy and toward the use of market type mechanisms.

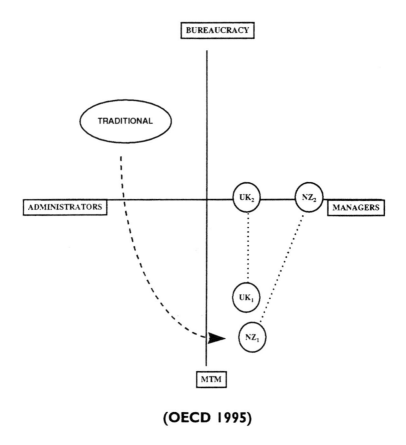

(OECD 1995)

In the second wave of reform, the unbridled emphasis on the market was modified in both the United Kingdom and New Zealand by a greater emphasis on local management and the introduction of service and performance standards. John Major's contribution was to institute Citizen's Charters, public service standards against which local citizens and clients could judge whether they were getting good service or value for their tax dollars. New Zealand contributed the theory of the Contract State, where direction and co-ordination of services were converted entirely to executive management contracts.

According to the OECD, these developments have now become a general trend across many countries. For example, the following graphic summarizes the developments in seven other countries, including Canada, since innovations were adopted in Britain and New Zealand.

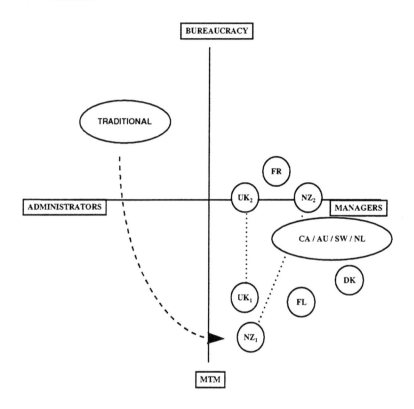

CA — Canada FR — France FL — Finland
NL — Netherlands DK — Denmark SW — Sweden
AU — Australia

(OECD 1995)

As shown, there has been a generalized trend away from centralized bureaucracy, at the top of the graphic, towards local management and new financial arrangements, allowing for variations between countries. Regardless of the legitimacy of other possible positioning for each country, the graphic clearly illustrates a movement across all countries toward the lower right quadrant.

In another frame on the same general developments, the OECD also looked at decentralization and decoupling of service delivery in the same seven countries. Again, though countries vary, all have moved away from the traditional structure, with decentralization as the more widespread phenomenon.

The other dimension of change is from integrated organizations that controlled both policy and service delivery, toward a "decoupled" system where policy functions are retained by central departments and service delivery decentralized or contracted out to others. The overall direction is away from public administration by centralized, integrated bureaucracies and toward decentralized, decoupled service delivery.

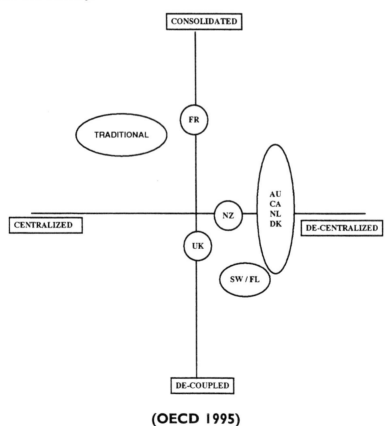

(OECD 1995)

The direction that began in Britain and New Zealand has now become a reference point for general changes. A whole range of public services, not just health, but education, general government services and social assistance are all undergoing alterations. We are witnessing a revolution in the theory and practice of public administration which will usher in a new era of public sector management.

What does this mean for public sector labour-management relations? Among these general winds of change, the decoupling, or split of purchaser and provider, will most destabilize public sector labour-management relations. Fiscal cuts and financial pressures can be handled in bargaining, but disaggregation and splits in service delivery and co-ordination amount to a fundamental threat to traditional approaches to wage determination, definition of union jurisdictions, bargaining units, job structures and work rules. The ground rules of who bargains for whom, over what and when, the fundamental fabric of collective agreements, will have to change.

The Debate on NPM: Passing Fad or Real Change?

The fiscal pressures facing governments today can not be met by traditional public sector managerial approaches. There is little doubt that a new managerial paradigm is necessary and it will draw on innovative government and private sector strategies. The New Public Management (NPM) offers a profound challenge to the status quo, by showing how private and public sector innovations can offer governments the ability to "do more with less" rather than simply cutting programs.

Not surprisingly, NPM has provoked considerable academic and political controversy. Nevertheless, NPM resists simple ideological bracketing: the question at hand is not simply big versus small government. It is how to transform government to deliver services in a more cost-effective and accountable manner. Because of its growing influence and major political impact on labour-management, it is useful to review recent studies of the New Public Management.

The NPM paradigm is best described as an "extended family" of inter-related ideas based on studies of successful public sector restructuring, and influenced by relevant innovations in private sector management. Pro-NPM commentator Sanford Borins (1994) has written an overview analysing new visions of public sector management.

In Osborne and Gaebler's widely read *Reinventing Government: How the Entrepreneurial Spirit is Transforming the Public Sector* (1992), ten principles that define the NPM are set out which Borins separates into two categories. Borins first groups principles that address internal management practices:

- individual public sector institutions should be mission — not rule — driven
- managers should identify and try to achieve measurable outputs, rather than concentrating on inputs
- service-delivery should meet the needs of stakeholders, not the internal needs of the bureaucracy
- problem-solving should be anticipatory and preventative, not reactive
- public sector management should be decentralized.

Borins offers a second category dealing with the proper relationship between private and public sectors:

- government should "steer not row," meaning that it should set policy but look to the private sector for service delivery
- governments should empower communities to take control over service delivery
- competition should be increased, with the private sector and within the public sector
- the public sector should be encouraged to earn, not only to spend
- governments should look to market incentives rather than new programs to solve problems.

The argument made here, somewhat different than Borins', is that the prime purpose in looking at reform experiments is not because privatization or markets will cure public sector problems. Rather, delivery will have to be made on a different cost and performance basis than at present.

The latest fad of Canadian public managers is Business Process Re-engineering, discussed earlier. However, in the private sector over seventy per cent (70%) of BPR projects fail to meet their objectives. The downsizing is so indiscriminant and demoralizing that productivity levels for the remaining staff fall through the floor. In the most extreme cases, a school board without students — they exist in New Jersey and Alberta — the organization no longer serves a useful purpose.

To retain a focus on values and purpose Robert Denhardt's *The Pursuit of Significance* (1993), outlines five principles that governments should follow:

- commitment to values
- serving the public
- empowering employees by encouraging participation and shared leadership
- recognizing that change occurs through pragmatic incrementalism
- employees dedicated to public service.

Denhardt does not emphasize the introduction of market-like mechanisms or competition between the public and private sectors. Instead, he argues that the two sectors are radically different. As long as public sector managers demonstrate the appropriate altruism and efficiency in implementing reforms, private sector competition should not be necessary.

In marked contrast, commentator Donald Savoie (1995a; 1995b) charges that NPM represents a rhetorical approach with ideological, almost religious, overtones. Rather than embracing a cross-fertilization of private and public sector management methods, he argues that the public sector faces unique challenges ignored by the NPM paradigm that preclude simple solutions. Savoie states that the two sectors are alike only in "unimportant ways" and finds the NPM literature is "strong on prescription and weak on diagnosis." In his view, the only real outcomes of NPM's conviction that private-sector practices are superior *and* applicable to government operations have been the enrichment of management consultants and declining public sector morale.

As an NPM critic, Savoie does not completely reject the need for change, but instead locates the main obstacles to fundamental reform at the political level, listing parliament, politicians, and public attitudes as the prime impediments to administrative reform.

Precisely because the public service *is* public, he sees little room for experimentation and even less latitude for error. Within the civil service, mistakes mean the possibility of intense public scrutiny and political pressure: politicians shoot first and ask questions later. There is little benefit to be gained by taking risks; competence and efficiency in the public sector is seldom rewarded. It is probably accurate to say that public sector managers labour under much greater political risks and accountabilities than the economic risks faced by their private sector counterparts.

In fact, Savoie is right when he argues that whereas "failure" and "success" in the private-sector are monitored by the discrete market process of consumer choice, citizens demand a high level of *public* accountability — a demand often mediated through the highly sensitive channels of the media and political process.

Politics will always play a role in service delivery in democratic societies. In real life, political needs of a government are not always well-served by encouraging clarity of mission. Political brokerage often means protecting contradictory objectives to increase spending flexibility; conflicting programs more often result from political influence than a lack of focus on the part of public sector managers. However, once budgets have been set and policy direction decided, cases of improved public sector management can be attributed to the creative energies of civil servants — a process driven by tighter budgets, improvements in computer technology, and simple common sense.

Yet, politicians in Canada are now recognizing that they face a much greater challenge in controlling state finances. Whereas the discipline of the capital market is felt directly and quickly by inefficient private sector organizations, the pressure on the public sector is indirect and cumulative because it affects the government as a collectivity. Nevertheless, that pressure is now politically recognized and is one of the primary drivers of the NPM paradigm. As a result of wide-spread public support for cost-saving reforms, political leaders are now demonstrating an increased level of support for bureaucratic innovation — even if reforms sometimes produce short-term embarrassments.

Finally, the charge that NPM is an extension of a neo-conservative ideology should not distract from current realities. Most nations, regardless of political inclination, recognize that the "growth model" of the 1970s and 1980s is a major cause of their current debt crises. The leading role played by social democratic administrations in New Zealand, Australia, Sweden, and Denmark in rethinking and reworking public sector service delivery supports this argument.

Whatever the final importance of NPM, change *is* taking place in the public sector. Front line managers and employees *are* responding to financial constraints and public expectations of better quality service. A more efficient public service does not mean that the traditional values associated with the civil service need be abandoned. In fact, three leading countries in public service reform — Australia, New Zealand, and the United Kingdom — have all recognized the need to rediscover the virtues of public service. The ultimate benchmarks of successful reform — greater productivity, longevity of reforms, and the replication of successful cases — do not necessarily conflict with established public sector standards.

While they may place a different emphasis on the importance of NPM as a model for change, commentators on both sides point with approval to the proliferation of successful reforms by various government departments and agencies, and stress the need for more analysis of real organizational transformations.

Public Sector Reform: A Look at Some Results

Recent research concludes that complete organizational turnarounds are a rare occurrence, most reforms are incremental in nature. Yet, Western Canada and Ontario seem to be generating a host of new managerial approaches.

International Survey: Canada, Sweden, U.S.

One study (Borins 1995) looked at eight cases of profound changes in line ministries and service agencies in Sweden, Canada, and the United States:
- Correctional Service of Canada (CSC)
- Archives of Ontario (Archives)

- U.S. Air Force Tactical Air Command (TAC)
- New York Department of Sanitation
- Bureau of Motor Equipment, Madison, Wisconsin (BME)
- Ontario Development Corporation (ODC)
- National Student Aid Board, Sweden (NSAB)
- Alberta (WCB) and Washington State (WCS) workers' compensation systems.

Six of these "turnarounds" were prompted by external pressure or review by the media, auditors, legislative committees, politicians, or public hearings. The two remaining cases developed because of internal pressure to reform: the Ontario Archives, in which restructuring was initiated in order to raise profile, and TAC. In all eight cases, changes were initiated by a new externally-recruited chief executive officer (CEO). These CEOs were "dynamic and energetic" and, all but one, were relatively young. Their success has been attributed to their leadership qualities and their familiarity with the business or stakeholders. In most cases, the new CEO made changes in the senior management team, replacing incumbents with managers committed to the reforms.

Regarding the content of the reforms, all the organizations reorganized work, and front-line staff, in particular, were encouraged to demonstrate creativity and make suggestions in this process. Information technology systems were used to improve management practices in five locations — Archives, CSC, ODC, NSAB, and WCB. Four involved decentralization, including identifying smaller units and giving these units a measure of autonomy. The study identifies a process of *reintegration* in five organizations, where formerly Tayloristic divisions of labour were replaced by multi-tasking. Broadening tasks served not only to reduce the alienation of staff from their work but, when combined with new case management systems, gave clients a closer relationship with front-line staff. Increased training and improvements in working conditions were also common remedies to address low morale and improve productivity.

In five cases, the organizations developed a new vision of themselves by drafting mission statements or strategic plans. In two institutions, the services delivered were better targeted — the ODC concentrated on lending to new technology-based firms and the WCB put more emphasis on rehabilitation. One institution, NSAB, embraced competition and aggressively sought and won additional responsibilities from other government agencies. The CSC, Archives, WCB, and WCS made significant efforts to reach out to their clients.

The Ontario Archives sought a higher profile in government through a tighter integration with its home ministry. Raising its profile helped the Archives secure funding and broaden its mandate to take on a new role implementing access to information legislation. In contrast, the ODC, WCB, and WCS sought greater autonomy from central government processes in order to establish more business-like operations. In all eight cases, reforms led to measurable financial or service improvements.

Service Quality B.C.

Service Quality B.C. was established as a special purpose central agency staffed by internally-recruited senior managers. It has a time-limited mandate to encourage the proliferation of a "post-bureaucratic paradigm" throughout the provincial government. The initiative has resulted in some notable outcomes including:

- Enquiry B.C., a toll-free telephone information system
- a plain-language guide to government services
- customer-service councils in various communities to help coordinate service-delivery
- a fifty per cent (50%) increase in productivity in Vancouver small claims courts
- a twelve per cent (12%) reduction in the cost of processing tax returns by introducing TQM principles.

Following the change in government in 1991, the agency's focus shifted from encouraging contracting out and privatization of government functions to winning labour support for the reforms. BC's approach has been copied in part by Quebec and Newfoundland and Labrador.

The Citizen's Charter, U.K.

In Great Britain, Prime Minister John Major has made a high profile personal commitment to implementing public sector reforms. Guided by public-choice economics, the cabinet secretariat has been introducing competition and contractual obligations throughout the public service. The Citizen's Charter approach establishes performance contracts between the public sector, on an organization-by-organization basis, and the public. In other words, the public sector works with consumers of government services. An examination of four charters indicates that while organizational self-definition and a better targeting of customer needs have been achieved, there have been few structural reorganizations, front-line staff have not been empowered, managers are generally not rewarded for improving performance, and there is some evidence of "Charter fatigue" within the public service. Changes in public sector culture and service delivery models raise the question whether traditional notions of ministerial accountability and the career civil service can survive the Charter process.

The Government Performance and Results Act, U.S.

In the United States, the *Government Performance and Results Act (GPRA)* is part of a coordinated government-wide reform of management and reporting practices. The *GPRA* requires all federal agencies to develop benchmarks to measure their performance, strategic goals, and to report to Congress and the President on their progress in meeting these goals. The legislative timeline began with seventy-one (71) pilot projects in fiscal 1994-1996, to be followed by government-wide implementation in the fall of 1997.

A recent General Accounting Office (GAO) report concentrates on the role of Congress and the President in the reform process. Strong and sustained congressional support for the *GPRA* is needed to reassure agency officials of ongoing political support. According to the GAO, the reporting relationship established by the *GPRA* encourages political decision-makers to address the problem of agencies whose missions are not well-defined, whose goals are unclear or nonexistent, and whose programs are not properly targeted. Such consultations will be helpful to Congress in modifying agencies' missions, setting better priorities, and restructuring or terminating programs.

While the Comptroller General is a strong supporter of these reforms, as befits an auditor, that office is also demanding and critical of the implementation process to date.

The testimony indicates that agencies — Environmental Protection Agency, Department of Energy, and Economic Development Administration — are beginning to realize that a focus on identifying measurable outcomes can dramatically increase their effectiveness. Program delivery presently suffers from a legacy of incremental and uncoordinated program growth, vague legislative mandates, overlapping responsibilities, and a lack of basic statistical data on program effectiveness. The GAO reports funding for employment assistance and training programs was $20 billion in 1995, spread across 163 programs in fifteen (15) agencies. A representative sample of these programs revealed that, in most cases, the basic statistical information needed to make informed management decisions was not available. Less than half the programs surveyed collected data on the subsequent success or failure of their former clients in the job market and only a quarter monitored the wages earned by those who found employment.

The report concludes with the following general questions that Congress should consider when communicating the importance of *GPRA* and when it assesses the status of agencies' implementation efforts:

- How well is the agency measuring outcomes?
- How are *GPRA* performance goals and information being used to drive the agency's daily operations?
- How is the agency using performance information to improve its effectiveness?
- What progress is the agency making in building the capacity necessary to implement *GPRA*?
- What steps is the agency taking to align its core business processes to support mission-related outcomes?

The Commonwealth Association of Public Administration and Management (CAPAM)

The experience of Commonwealth nations is surveyed in a 1994 report for the Commonwealth Association of Public Administration and Management (CAPAM). This report summarizes papers presented to the inaugural conference of CAPAM on the subject of administrative reform. It argues that the ultimate goal of new managerial practices should be to increase the freedom of self-expression and material well-being of the populations they serve, and identifies five general goals for public sector reforms:

- ***Governments should provide high-quality services that citizens value***
  Specific initiatives include: mechanisms for increasing customer feedback, one-stop shopping for government services, and the introduction of total quality management programs. John Major's Citizens Charter approach has been emulated in New Zealand, Malaysia, and Namibia.
- ***Managers need increased autonomy from central agency control***
  Various countries have implemented a degree of separation between policy development and program-delivery. This and other reforms have introduced a greater flexibility for managers and front-line staff. Australia and New Zealand have addressed employment rigidities by increasing parental leave, part-time work, and "flex-time" arrangements. In Australia and the U.K., there has been a shift from government-wide collective bargaining to workplace bargaining. In New Zealand, private sector employment law has been applied to the public sector allowing staff to nominate their own bargaining agents and, in addition to collective agreements, introducing the possibility of individual work contracts.
- ***Organizations and individuals should be measured and rewarded for meeting performance goals***
  Fixed-term contracts and performance agreements are replacing tenure for senior managers. New Zealand has reduced the demand for new capital by charging departments

for their borrowing requirements. As well, New Zealand and the U.K. have moved from cash to accrual accounting. Australia's embrace of mission statements, fiscal targets, competition, and benchmarking has resulted in annual ten per cent (10%) increases in labour productivity from 1987 to 1992, a twenty-four per cent (24%) reduction in air travel and international long-distance calling costs, and a growth in the state-owned sector's profitability from $170 million (AUD) in 1988-89 to $5.2 billion in 1993-94. On-going program reviews are also being introduced by other countries surveyed.

- *Human and technological resources need to be fully marshalled by managers to meet performance targets*
Singapore presents the most compelling example of this principle. Information technology upgrading has resulted in a return of $2.71 for every dollar invested and has made 5,000 public service positions redundant. The city-state also puts great emphasis on recruitment, locating the most-talented university students and subsidizing their education at home and abroad in return for the promise of government service after graduation. Both Singapore and the U.K. have instituted customer service training for their staff. Employment equity programs were also seen favourably by many participants as programs to expand the pool of available talent and address systematic inequalities. Various member countries have restructured central agencies and their interaction with line departments, raising the profile of public sector restructuring, rationalizing the number and roles of departments, and changing the role of central agencies from direct control over inputs to coordinating and guiding the reform process throughout government.

- *An open-minded attitude toward competition, within the public service and with the private sector*
The U.K. has seen an increase in the procurement of market-tested goods from £25 million to £1.3 billion between 1992 and 1994, with an estimated savings of twenty per cent (20%) or more. Where the public sector has retained service delivery contracts, the threat of competition has generated

additional cost savings. Countries have also increased their reliance on private sector financing of infrastructure projects and non-governmental service delivery. Privatization has been pursued in Singapore (telecom, airline, and shipyards), the U.K. (forty-seven privatization initiatives since 1979), Zimbabwe (partial privatization of the IMF-imposed Structural Adjustment Program), as well as Ghana, Tanzania, New Zealand, and Malta. Deregulation and industrial strategies are additional examples of private-public sector cooperation.

Linking Measurement and Management

Canada, like most federal states, has a very large set of transfer payments. Transfers occur between different levels of government and between governments and operating agencies such as hospitals, schools and social agencies. Canadian provincial governments cannot manage a reform process without introducing a new form of differential transfer payments and operating grants for local authorities. The present system contains reverse incentives. Take two hospitals in the same city: one, with progressive management has improved their costs, worked out a new deal with their unionized employees and new service delivery systems; the other has changed nothing in twenty years, the same approaches and inefficiencies remain. Under the current system, both hospitals receive the same flat operating grants. In the past, it was felt that there was no way to introduce new directions into the system except by layering in new funding. This worked to a limited degree — hospital funding in Ontario increased eleven per cent (11%) annually throughout the 1980s. Now, with the total spending envelope at best, frozen, and likely to contract over the next five years, central governments, have no evident, sensible way out except by starting to differentiate operating grants based on performance. This does not mean that all dollars will or should be conditional on outcome indicators, but a substantial portion must be. This is what is meant by *performance-based government*.

It is neither possible nor desirable to base everything on one system of measurement. Nor will it be a matter of simply introducing industrial efficiency, measuring outputs against inputs as in private sector manufacturing. Measures of productivity in the public sector must involve measures of effectiveness: outcomes, not outputs. It is always possible to boost efficiency by laying people off and cutting services. But this will not be an acceptable outcome where community expectations remain high. Outcome measures must be complex, more than a single measurement. This complexity is what makes current controversies about measuring school board performance through public release of school marks both the right and the wrong question. Taxpayers and parents have every right to expect explicit information on how the school system is performing. The stand by teachers' unions across the country against release of marks is not likely to succeed, nor should it. On the other hand, teacher groups are correct in arguing that we cannot simply look at school grades in the abstract. We rightly have a variety of outcomes we expect from the school system, and need a variety of measurements to reflect both school performance and comparative performance between boards. Techniques for building high performance school systems are under discussion from the Netherlands to New South Wales.

Across the public sector, performance indicators are being introduced as part of service management as well as in the budget process.

Proposed New Funding Formula for Ontario Hospitals

At the micro-economic level, an example of what is likely to come is the development of a new hospital allocation formula in Ontario. Through a sub-committee of the Ministry of Health's Joint Policy and Planning Committee (JPPC) a new Hospital Allocation Formula was developed in 1993-94. The purpose of the formula was to develop a set of thirteen hospital performance indicators that would re-allocate a portion of the hospital budgets. In the proposed new system, our two hypothetical hospitals above might receive more or less than the normative grant, based on their performance or outcomes. The process of developing the criteria involved the government, hospital and external representatives and is designed as ongoing. The new scheme specifically allows for future revisions of its content, as well as an appeals process for disputes over the specific application and fiscal outcome.

The committee decided in favour of a rate-based funding approach where standard payment rates are established for the provision of standard patient services. A major consideration in the new direction was the impact of funding information feedback on hospital management. The new scheme creates a conceptual shift in the management responsibility, from the funder to the provider. This rate-based system forces hospitals to make tough management decisions, focusing more on defining their "product lines" and reducing their costs, and spending less time contesting reimbursement rates. Costs become more a management and less a funding issue. The former, cost-based funding system, by contrast, puts more responsibility on the funder, who may be lobbied to provide additional dollars to cover costs incurred. Hospitals will now be preoccupied with actual input costs.

The new funding formula allocates resources to hospitals based on projected service volume levels and establishes prospective funding rates for different patient activity areas such as inpatient acute, emergency, psychiatry, pediatrics, long-term care, rehabilitation, daycare and clinics.

Governance issues also weigh heavily in the new approach. The proposed formula is more responsive to service changes at the individual hospital level. The rate system provides a provincial standard which can be adjusted for unique provider characteristics. The formula ensures responsiveness to service volume changes without micro-managing individual hospitals. Hospitals would contract with the Ministry of Health concerning aggregate volumes of service, based on the needs of their referral population. The accountability of hospital boards would shift from an emphasis on the responsible spending of a given amount of resources to an emphasis on meeting the service needs of their population, increasing the accountability of hospital boards and local management.

Macro-Level Performance Indicators

At the macro-economic level, governments are looking to broad social indices for direction on where social development should be focused and for objectives against which current performance and progress can be measured. The introduction and implementation of performance measurement systems within and outside of the budget process constitute a major change to the public sector landscape in the 1990s. These systems are not likely to fall off the table, even with changes of government, because they represent an important part of a larger metamorphosis in the public sector from *managing inputs* to *management of outputs and outcomes.*

Performance reporting may be used as part of the budget process, as part of annual reports, or as broad social indicators. These uses share the common objective of better informing decision-makers and the public on what the taxpayers are getting for their money. To date, development of such indicators has been restricted primarily to government policy shops, advanced local management groups and consultants. Public awareness and discussion of indicators and their implications will grow in the years ahead as they are more directly related to the decision-making process.

In the United States, the previously-noted *Government Performance and Reporting Act* of 1994 gives all agencies of the United States government five years to develop:

- performance measurement indicators for all their activities
- performance plans for implementation
- annual published performance reports.

The power of American political examples means that standards set in the U.S. may well be adopted by other governments. In Australia, over the last five years special performance reports have become regular annual features of the auditor general. For instance, in Western Australia, in addition to an annual report on financial statements of all public agencies, the auditor general publishes a separate performance report on the complete public sector. Similar requirements may well be forthcoming in Canada.

The Oregon Benchmarks are among the best known of the broad social indicators for the public sector. These social indices and general public sector objectives are designed to orient government, agencies and the public, to the long-run social objectives of the Oregon state government. They include broad targets — literacy rates, levels of homelessness, family violence, water and air quality

— to be achieved in Oregon over a ten-year period. The province of Alberta has introduced proposed performance indicators, in part derived from the experiences of the Oregon Benchmarks.

It is critical to distinguish the objective of any performance measurement system. One set of measures may be relevant to the budget process. Another can be used to benchmark organizational efficiency and effectiveness for purposes of improvement over time. Yet another is for broad social goal-setting as demonstrated in Oregon. Local management and employee groups need focused delivery and cost-related indicators. But, these will be ineffective without the broad Oregon style social benchmarks for context, political decision-making and public participation.

A Caution on Performance Indicators (PIs)

Starting from some crisis, perhaps accompanied by a change in authority figures, the desire for new measures to make the system more accountable is awakened. Once conscious the process moves through various phases in which PIs are chosen and as a result of attention and management action an early improvement in performance is witnessed. As obvious improvements are exhausted and managers have a better grasp of how the indicators work, there is an incentive to manipulate the system to maintain the required rate of improvement. This "gaming" often takes the form of attention to measured activities at the expense of tasks which are less well-defined or measured. Attempts to correct this distortion can lead to a proliferation of indicators. In a formalized and complex system which is so difficult to understand certain activities fall into disuse, as attention shifts to other concerns within the organization.

Source: Kieron Walsh, *Public Services and Market Mechanisms: Competition, Contracting and the New Public Management.*

Performance-based Challenges to Labour-Management Relations

Performance-based government will have an impact on labour-management relations in two particular areas: decentralization and explicit productivity tradeoffs.

If, through decentralization, transfer revenues are related to individual, local organizational performance, then wage-setting in the broad public sector will be significantly altered. In the past, wage determination has either been very centralized in province-wide master contracts covering, for example, hospitals or schools, or it has been the subject of arbitration, tightly following industry patterns and comparabilities. While there may still be general trends in a decentralized public sector, much more emphasis will shift to local issues and agreements. At a particular hospital, for instance, if economic performance becomes a prime determinant of revenues, it may not be able to "afford" the centrally-set wage patterns. And even where wages are set centrally, local rules on work organization, job classification and employee assignment flexibility will become much more important. Either way, local agreements will take greater precedence over central negotiations. This will particularly challenge the centralist tendencies within public sector trade unions.

As local organizations reconfigure to meet their community needs and markets, local human resource management issues will take on much greater importance in order to seek explicit productivity tradeoffs in bargaining. Wage demands will have to be offset by local productivity and service improvements. Where, in the past, a nurse might only have done "nursing" work, we may have nurses fulfilling a number of different roles, such as coordinator of a multi-skilled service team. Local parties will now have to negotiate tradeoffs of a new kind. In the near term, there probably will be re-configurations of benefits, various scheduling premiums, bonuses and leave provisions. Total compensation levels will involve tradeoffs between wages, benefits and jobs. Later, job combinations and work team assignments will consolidate existing multiple job classifications and lead to simplified work rules. To negotiate in the old way — standard labour costs — will mean that the parties wind up negotiating layoffs. It will be in their mutual self-interest to negotiate new individual productivity tradeoffs.

"De-Inventing Government" — New Zealand Comes to Alberta

Alberta is the subject of one of the most radical experiments to "de-invent" government. The Ralph Klein vision is of a smaller government and public service. This concept is much more than simple radio hotline political rhetoric. As indicated by interviews with senior government officials and academic commentators, it is motivated by the model of government originating with the Labour Government in New Zealand a decade ago, the previously-mentioned Contract State. More than anything else, this transformation in the basic model of government will alter what it means to be a civil servant.

In the Contract State model of the public sector, the core functions of government are in policy and strategy development, not service delivery. In a strategic change, government will no longer be a dominant provider of services, but a purchaser of services where required. Existing government service delivery will be contracted out more and more. When there is an over-riding policy requirement to do so, contracting-in of services and people will occur.

The overall direction for Alberta was defined in the 1993 budget study, *New Approaches to Government*. The scenario of development in the Alberta public sector over the past several years is at least a possible script for the rest of the country, particularly the Harris Conservatives in Ontario. In stage one, fiscal reductions and balancing the budget dictated across-the-board fiscal cutbacks. In stage two, business plans were developed in each of the core government businesses for three years, which included a twenty-five per cent (25%) reduction in staff. In stage three, with a balanced budget in view, the question becomes what business does the government want to be for the long term? Does it have "employees" and if so, what do they do? What will it mean to be a civil servant? In skills profiles there will be both specialists, with more generic high-end technical skills than at present, and generalists. A dependency on networks with interpersonal and communications skills will be much more important for teams, leaders and contractor administrators. Pay will also be decentralized to departments with broad banding and bonuses will be given out of savings beyond the fiscal targets.

All this means a significant alteration in the skills of civil servants. Civil servants need more contract management abilities and improved assessment and evaluation skills. Within the Alberta government there is substantial debate about whether policy should be carried out by dedicated specialists or by generalists overseeing development of policy by outside specialists. The underlying message is clear: government will be in the policy and contracting business. Service delivery skills will be a declining component of the government skills inventory.

How much should or can be contracted out? Advocates of contract-based management argue that funding, and therefore the cost of public services, becomes transparent in this approach. Identification of objectives and performance measures in contracts enable evaluation of the outcomes from public expenditure. Separating the political process of determining objectives and specifying public services from delivery will make professionals more responsive to the needs of users. Public choice theory and principal-agent theory provide the theoretical bases for the two arguments:

- private competitive markets are better than political markets (government hierarchies) in supplying goods and services to the community
- contracts are better mechanisms for accountability than internal organizational control, based on budgets.

Public choice theorists argue for privatization of as much government activity as possible. Principal-agent theorists are not so much concerned with ownership as the mode of delivery of public services. They argue for contracting out as much of the public sector as possible.

Alberta is now experimenting with "special operating agencies," generic internal agencies that compete to deliver services. Senior officials and ministers actively debate what services can be converted to private businesses. Numerous jails and correctional services have been privatized in U.S. — is this the future for Canada? Contracting out of regulatory affairs is possible: Alberta is developing independent delivery organizations called Delegated Regulatory Organizations (DROs). The Ministry of Labour has turned over the inspection of boilers and pressure vessels to private contractors or DROs. The board of the DRO is a public trust, a body to oversee the public interest. The process of experimentation with divested delivery agencies will obviously continue.

The Alberta Treasury Board has already privatized the government's payroll operations. In Alberta, improved efficiency is the goal, achievable through a competitive environment pushing government to change. The problem is not that Albertans are lazy. It is that for in-house services, there are no measures or tests for efficiency. The system grew larger and larger, and is perceived as having become increasingly inefficient as it grew. In the Treasury view, this can be corrected through a contract-based "market" in government services.

In the Alberta view, the fundamental socio-economic situation has changed since the 1950s. The public service now has much greater capacity to decentralize. The availability of new information technology reinforces the government's political choices. It can implement its policy objectives in new ways, without the traditional command and control mechanisms of central bureaucracies. Across the economy, there has been a fundamental change for all employment relations, a flattening of the management structure. It has come late to the public sector but the impacts may be more profound. For government, there was extreme reliance on paper-based technology and authority to convey and enforce decisions. Now messages are conveyed, implemented and monitored electronically by computer. The 1905 *Alberta Public Sector Act* set up rigid job classifications and hiring procedures as part of public administration reform and to eliminate corruption. Now much of this is regarded as physically not necessary. As a result, a hierarchy of labour-management relations was implemented in the public sector with work rules, job classes and other features. Now there is a general ability to accomplish work outside the core corporation. The government used to own its own buildings, but not now, there is no need. Nor is it necessary for government to process pay cheques, benefit cheques, income tax claims, and so on. Technology can assure the outcomes without the government owning the capital or the employees. The primary need is for management of overall standards and strategic policy capability.

Alberta learned from New Zealand, where government departments run as separate corporations. There, in the Contract State, all government departments are independent contracting agencies whose services are purchased by the central government body. Alberta has not moved as far, but a New Zealand framework is the logical conclusion to the developments underway and the conceptual framework that has been adopted.

Labour-Management Relations and the Contract State

For labour-management relations observers, the technology issue is getting confused with other, emotional, issues such as contracting out or union busting. In fact the re-organization of service delivery is much more like the transformation in leasing of capital equipment in the private sector in the 1970s. The United States already has an active market in "leased employees" with a company specializing in it called The Employee Leasing Company. Entrepreneurs dedicated to leasing public service employees are not out of the question in the future of the Canadian public sector. The combination of the theory of the Contract State and the availability of new technologies that facilitate the implementation of the theory is potentially the biggest challenge to what being a civil servant employee has historically meant, both for the individual and for the bargaining agent. It threatens existing bargaining relations and bargaining power. In this respect, what is going on in the public sector is even more challenging than the 1980s crisis in private sector industrial relations. The 1980s saw a challenge to transform labour-management relations in the face of industrial competition, i.e. new Japanese manufacturing models, new technology and human resource management. But in all these cases, private business stayed in business. In the Contract State, government may simply exit the business of service delivery.

Contracting out is among the most volatile labour-management issues. The underlying concern is the right of employees who have been providing the service work to continue to do so; a right that is often written into existing collective agreements. Contracting out of work has been increasingly tempting for management as a means to achieve short-term cost savings. In reply, unions try to make the current contract rules as rigid as possible.

Contracting out, in the common industrial relations sense, has been and it will continue to be present in labour-management relations. However, this is the smaller part of the emerging overall story. Contracting, along the lines of the contract state model, will become a pervasive and ambient part of the operating environment across the public sector in the years to come. There will be contracting in, out and between as various boundaries on the organization change. Improvements in productivity and service delivery will lead to new arrangements between public and private sector partners and between different operating agencies within the public sector. It is not a simple matter of in versus out, or public versus private.

In the Dutch municipal sector, for example, "inter-communal" arrangements have become commonplace. Legally and politically separate and independent municipalities share services; one does the payroll for all, another does the streets, another the garbage collection. In the Finnish municipal sector, International Standards Organization (ISO) 9000 standards are being introduced for delivery of municipal services just as they have been for private industry. A special manual has been created to assist municipal agencies drawing up contracts for procurement of public services from suppliers in stipulating quality provisions in the services provided.

The more important question about contracting out is how contracting fits into the general business strategy of the organization and its model for service delivery. For instance, local hospital management might save a dollar or two by competitively bidding its cleaning contract. However, this will probably have adverse effects on employee morale for the rest of the staff. Alternatively, the best long-term strategy for improved cost, productivity, and quality of service, might include the re-engineering of functions so that the cleaners are not off in a separate entity (contracted-out or not) but instead form an integral part of the service delivery team involving patient-care teams of multi-skilled service workers assigned to various wards and patient groups. The latter structure, which brings more long-term benefits, is not best-suited to using contract employees.

The Purchaser-Provider Split and Labour-Management Relations

Because of its sheer size, fiscal weight and community service needs, the health system is the leading case for macro-level public sector restructuring. The stereotypical case is defined by the precedent of the Thatcher government in the U.K. splitting the purchaser and provider functions in the National Health Service (NHS). The objective was to create an "internal market" for the supply of health services, by separating the provision of health care services from the purchase of those services.

In the post-Thatcher reformed NHS, government funds are provided to two basic provider groups: District Health Authorities and General Practitioner (GP) Fundholders. Private medical insurers, private health care organizations and private individuals can compete with the public bodies to provide services. The main providers are new trust status hospitals and those hospitals that have remained with the District Authority. Some GP Fundholders are moving to provide routine services, such as minor surgery, in-house. The Thatcher initiative was followed by Prime Minister Major's declaration of Citizen's and Patient's Charters stating minimum service performance guarantees.

A detailed discussion of the British NHS reforms and funding is not possible here. The relevant principal is the movement towards a model where the government takes less of a delivery role and more of a funding and performance standards role. No government in Canada has gone as far as the government in the UK. However, the basic model of government being used in Alberta and New Zealand discussed previously, inevitably invites implementation of such a scheme.

Two practical outcomes are in evidence for labour-management relations. Within government operations themselves, the model of questioning what business the government is in, is driving Alberta in the direction of the contractual state. The practical implications are massive downsizing of the civil service, leaving a remaining core of specialists in policy development, contract management and performance measurement skills. Vast contracting out would follow as the government moves towards either being a contracting employer or not a major employer at all. Both of these challenge the traditional conception of the civil servant with long service, narrow bureaucratic skills and institutional continuity in service delivery.

A feature of the U.K. model being implemented in Canada is in the management of the health care system. This is to have regionalized boards responsible for the health delivery system. Across the country, whether they are called District Health Councils, Regional Health Authorities or Regional Health Boards, there is a broad move to shift responsibility for health outcomes and, eventually, allocation of health care dollars away from centralized Ministries of Health and towards local authorities. Whether or not the experiment is ever taken as far as the British purchaser-provider split, the move to devolve authority is having some of the same effects.

The industrial relations implications of regionalization are already emerging. Issues are arising such as determination of who the employer is, successor rights, whether former employees of a ministry are transferred and if so, where and with what contractual conditions, seniority and employment security rights. Overall, this will challenge the relatively centralized process of health and hospital-based collective bargaining that has characterized the past quarter century. Regionalization efforts in health in Saskatchewan, Alberta and B.C. are all bogged down with unresolved employment relations issues. Movements to decentralize authority, management and finances are destabilizing health sector labour-management relations. This may be a precursor to, or even become a metaphor for, future public sector labour-management relations generally.

Employment Relations and Re-Engineering Delivery Systems

Re-engineering efforts affecting local organizations, such as hospitals and municipalities, have become pervasive across the country.

Given that this is where the vast majority of public dollars and services are actually expended, and where the overwhelming majority of public workers are employed, what happens at the local institutional level will have immense effects on the outcomes for employment relations. It is also at this level that the most contentious labour contractual issues are likely to arise.

While there are as many different approaches to re-engineering as there are clients and consultants, the directions of development converge around several core themes. Current services are being re-examined to find ways to reduce costs and improve the quality and effectiveness of service. Because seventy to eighty per cent (70-80%) of expenses are generated by the wage bill, restructuring of service delivery entails re-allocations of skill and labour. This requires a move away from the traditionally separate, functional entities and silos, each with their own separate administrative structure, self-contained job classifications and often their own collective agreements.

The following graphics offer a stylized representation of the traditional and the new organizational structures that are typical of local restructuring and re-engineering efforts in the hospital and municipal fields. The labour-management issues that flow from even these relatively simple re-designs are complex and contentious. First, there are often separate bargaining units corresponding to these separate entities. In the municipal field, the waterworks could easily be represented by the Operating Engineers, while the office and permits group could be represented by two separate CUPE locals. If the group merged what collective agreement would it be under? How would job re-definition and work reorganization be reconciled with the three separate collective agreements, each with its own job classification and work rules? Similarly, the divisions between police and firefighters, each with its own union, separate collective agreement and, in most provinces, separate legislation and arbitration system, would have to be re-aligned. There are already issues concerning the intersection of jurisdiction between paramedics and firefighters, uniformed police officers and civilianization of police service boards.

Traditional Hospital Structure

```
         Board of Directors & CEO

Medical   Nursing   Surgery   Program   Human        Finance
Staff                         Support   Resources
```

Integrated Services Hospital

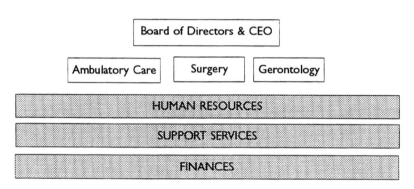

Traditional Municipal Structure

```
         Board of Directors & CEO

Medical   Nursing   Surgery   Program   Human        Finance
Staff                         Support   Resources
```

Integrated Services Municipality

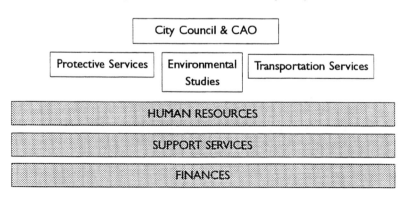

In the hospital field, the movement towards patient-focused care is being resisted by a number of unions. Moves toward merging work on the wards where nurses with expanded-roles lead work teams of multi-skilled service workers and technicians, raises boundary questions about separate nurse, technician and service-worker bargaining units, job classifications and work rules. In the other direction, in most provinces, movements to expand the case management and diagnostic roles of nurses raise issues about the boundaries of practice defined by health disciplines legislation and regulations. Just as job classifications in labour contracts have expanded in the 1980s, so also have the number of self-regulated professional groups under the health disciplines legislation. The related challenge for health sector industrial relations is the general movement away from dependence on acute care hospital services and towards more community-based health services.

Labour-Management Relations in a Shifting Managerial Environment

There has been a distinct lack of attention in NPM studies and from commentators to the consequences of unionization in the public sector. The complexities involved in seeking employee buy-in for reforms — especially relevant to the Canadian context — are referred to only tangentially. Some of the accumulated institutional obstacles to increased productivity, such as job-control unionism, fragmented bargaining units, and the upward pressure on wages, are dealt with briefly, if at all. The precise objective of various NPM reforms — fiscal savings, finding measurable benchmarks of public sector efficiency, or meeting broader social policy goals — are not always identified. Neither are the possible conflicts between these different objectives explored. Nonetheless, labour-management relations in the public sector will increasingly be impacted by performance-based government, both in the budget allocation process and at the local level in setting productivity and service goals.

Bob Hebdon is one critic who does address labour-management relations in *The Perils of Privatization: Lessons for New York State*. Hebdon points out the market theories which underlie privatization posit organized labour as a barrier to "true" competition. With few exceptions, the privatization literature he surveys ignores the potential role for unions in negotiating contracting out and does not consider the historical development of public sector bargaining.

For instance, in New York state, which has a higher rate of unionization than Ontario, and more union members in total than the Canadian Labour Congress (CLC), the Taylor Law (1967) was introduced during a period of considerable social unrest including numerous illegal public service strikes. The new law provided industrial peace by introducing a formal bargaining regime and enforceable penalties against striking public sector workers and unions. An implicit "social contract" ensured that, in return for stability, workers could use the new law to advance their economic interests. Hebdon suggests that in the New York situation, shifting public sector work to the private sector may recreate the same conditions of labour unrest — especially given differences between private and public sector labour law with the right to strike — that led to the introduction of this law in the first place.

With or without an adequate theoretical underpinning or academic study of the likely impact, public sector labour-management relations are being frog-marched into the future under the banner of New Public Management. Comprising an unstated bundle of objectives, techniques and histories, the effects of NPM on labour-management relations will unfold in one organization and sector at a time. The dynamics of this future-history in hospitals, municipalities and at Ontario Hydro are considered in the following chapters.

— CHAPTER 3 —
FAD, PHASE OR FUTURE?
Managerialism in Health Care

Canada's accessible, tax-supported Medicare system has made health care the largest expenditure in most provincial budgets, and the health care sector the largest single public sector employer. An aging population and increasing costs of care have produced demand for greater efficiency within the health care delivery system and the beginning of a long push for health care reform. While unionization rates vary — about ninety per cent (90%) of those eligible in acute care hospitals and seventy per cent (70%) of all employees — it is on the unionized workforce that this pressure has most come to bear. What happens in health care reform will have a substantial impact on reform of public sector labour-management relations across the board.

Health care reform's regionalization and wellness thrusts provide opportunity and encouragement for government to reduce the traditionally strong reliance upon adversarialism in labour-management relations. Regionalism and wellness are both strong components of a broad democratic objective. But, meaningful labour relations reform can occur only through shifting to explicitly participatory arrangements which treat workers and their unions as stakeholders and partners in the reform process. On the other hand, the magnitude of the changes, a poor existing industrial relations climate in the health care sector — witness repeated nurses' strikes in Alberta, Manitoba, Quebec and Nova Scotia in recent years — combined with drastic cuts in health care budgets does not provide an amiable environment for diminishing adversarialism. Most unions involved in health care across the country are highly suspicious of the motives of governments and employers' associations. Unions are waging a defensive battle for their members' job security, while at the same time expressing grave concerns about deteriorating services.

Two models of health care reform and its impact on labour-management relations are already becoming evident. In Alberta, downsizing appears to be taking place in the most drastic manner. Government is withdrawing massive funding without a central plan, without consultation with unions and with little consultation with management as well. In this "slash and burn" model, the parties are left to adjust in whatever "voluntary" manner they can.

In contrast, British Columbian health care reform has involved a high degree of planning and consultation between all stakeholders. B.C. demonstrates managed change, active policies to assist displaced workers and shared transitions. This suggests positive benchmarks for transition, which, for example, Saskatchewan is trying to duplicate. It merits noting that B.C.'s buoyant economy to date has provided money and time that other governments may not have available. The real test for the British Columbia model will come with the attempted redeployment of workers from the acute care sub-sector to the "outer" health care sub-sector of long term care and community care services. This outer area is characterized by much lower union density and wages than acute care. Union jurisdictional lines are much less clear. Employers in the outer area, whether for-profit — albeit from government funds — or small, perennially under-funded not-for-profits, have not been union-friendly organizations. It will be very difficult to get these employers to accept the terms of any framework agreement without radically altering the entire structure and funding of the outer sector.

Lessons from Britain's National Health Service

The first phase of change in the NHS, in the late 1970s and early 1980s, was a determined unilateral drive to impose greater economy and efficiency through direct government fiscal reductions and unilateral institution of performance measures. Cost-consciousness, fiscal savings and the dissemination of the skills of financial management were the leading characteristics of changes introduced in many public services. In the NHS, "cost improvement programmes" became a feature of daily life, and the planning process turned from longer-term strategy towards tightly costed short-term operational plans.

The second phase in the later 1980s and early 1990s saw the introduction of more indirect, new, management-led techniques of professional employee involvement and work place reform of service delivery. Efforts for quality improvement, cultural change and a major extension of market and market-type mechanisms were now added to the emphasis on economy and efficiency. Monolithic public service provision was replaced by relatively small purchasing organizations buying from a variety of service providers.

The prognosis is that in the new system, managerial authority will expand and job security for all occupational groups will shrink. Efficiency and responsiveness will increase and decision-making will become more transparent. One commentator has questioned whether the positive elements for people working in the system in the vision of the second wave of public sector managerialism as reflected in *Working for Patients* and the *Patient's Charter* will come to pass (Pollitt 1994, 1995).

In the first wave of managerial reform in the NHS, the introduction of general managers was judged to have brought substantially more control over non-medical health professionals than the previous system of administration. However, while management pronouncements and "initiatives" were plenty, relatively little of substance was achieved at the level of service delivery. This was particularly the case in the area of patient health "consumerism."

Introduction of Performance Indicators (PIs)

The introduction of performance indicators is at the forefront of forced-paced change in Alberta and Ontario. Analysts of the British experience (Horizon and Pollitt 1994) suggest that authorities advocating the use of performance measurement systems should seek to:
- establish a consensus on the basis for the comparison of performance between different organizations using strategies such as working groups and creating a set of guidelines for implementation
- establish standardized information systems and definitions of work systems as the basis of the indicators and comparisons

- identify a small number of key measures of performance to give general guidelines instead of micro-management.

Incorporation of Professionals

The direct involvement of health professionals in management of the new system has been central to the NHS changes. One of the major NHS devices for incorporation of professionals into the new system of hospital management has been the establishment of Clinical Directorates, referred to in Canada as Programme Management. In the "Johns Hopkins Model" — in use in the NHS — the hospital is constituted into a number of "clinical units," defined in terms of specialty. Each unit is managed by a medically qualified chief with a small management team comprised of the chief, a nurse director and an administrator. This team has a budget, is accountable for direct costs, and is, in principle, able to chose between the purchase of centrally-provided catering, cleaning and maintenance services and purchase outside the hospital. In this model, the hospital becomes a kind of holding company. This has allowed each service unit to be managed as a separate "business unit" with reductions in administrative and overhead charges, improving efficiency.

Quality

In the NHS the predominant concepts of quality remain professional — medical and nursing audits — and where they are not professional they are mostly managerial. Patients are certainly consulted more often than in the past but the consultations are usually on management's terms. They are frequently asked what they think of the offered services or how they themselves would define and assess quality. What is more, they are asked for their opinions but are in no way empowered to ensure that notice is taken of their views once expressed. Total quality management may be built around the notion of "fitness for purpose" but the data collected on patients' purposes is still very thin. Ticking the boxes on a management-designed patient satisfaction questionnaire is a long way short of "services geared to the requirements of patients."

Managerialist Strategies: Unilateralism v. Incorporation

The third leg of the stool in NHS managerialism was a direct challenge to the unions representing the NHS workforce. Changes to the rule of work demarcation between occupations have been critical to the new "managerial" relations in the NHS. A long-established pattern has been to transfer routine "unskilled" elements of professionals' work to less or unqualified subordinate groups such as nursing assistants or physiotherapy aides. A qualitative change in nursing has occured, where semi-skilled health care assistants are able to undertake a good deal of nursing work but are not subject to national licensing requirements or national pay bargaining arrangements. On the other side, there are processes of differentiation within the nursing profession. Drives toward increased educational and professional qualifications has created a continuous shift towards degree-level nursing and beyond. The anticipated result is that, in future, there will be a core of highly-qualified, highly-paid nurses, supported by a flexible, inexpensive peripheral work force. Some commentators perceive this polarization of the nursing work body as enhancing its controllability by management, a path they expect other health professions to follow. North American practices converging on "patient-centred" care with registered nurses anchoring a team of multi-skilled lower paid assistants has formalized this development.

Much of what is currently happening in Canada — particularly in Alberta and Ontario — is "backing into the future" along the lines already established in Britain. As seen in the U.K., the majority of health care will still be delivered under the umbrella of the public system. But, the intense, budget-driven changes in Canada are propelling us more directly into NHS stage three, placing the labour issues at the top of the chart.

The Ontario Public Health System

At present Ontario is experiencing a simultaneous introduction of both fiscal reductions and performance measures. A draconian forced march of aggregate reductions in fiscal transfer payments to hospitals has begun along with the "consultative" introduction of performance measures linked to transfer reductions. At the micro-level, individual hospital management is seeking to engage their workforces and trade unions in collaborative process of work re-organization and employee empowerment.

However, this consultation and employee group involvement, of a limited kind, are happening at the local level, *outside* the collective bargaining process. Collective bargaining is centralized between the Ontario Hospital Association (OHA) and union head offices. Both the OHA and the centrals are being marginalized in the process. The new linkage of transfer payments with performance will have the weight of the law of gravity in centralized bargaining until something gives and a new configuration emerges.

Performance Indicators in Ontario

For some time, the Ontario hospital sector struggled with on-going issues related to the flat-rate operating grant formula that calculated government funding allocations to hospitals and the need for a mechanism to deal with re-allocation within a fixed fiscal envelope. The system, based on historical costs, did not provide local hospital administration with incentives for improvement or rewards for innovation. A Joint Policy and Planning Committee (JPPC) of the Ministry of Health and the hospital industry association, the Ontario Hospital Association (OHA), was formed. And, in 1992, the Hospital Funding Committee (HFC) of the JPPC was charged with developing a methodology to deal with reallocation of hospital funding resources. The HFC set up working groups on adjustment factors, activity measurement, funding integration and data quality.

To deal with the wide diversity of hospitals in the system — teaching, community, urban, rural, large, small, specialized — the JPPC defined a set of peer groups to level out these differences. Peer groups are used for comparison purposes and based on the number of beds and teaching status. Peer groups were developed as an interim approach for a fair comparison of like hospitals, considering the limitations of the cost-weighted case calculation. The average for each peer group was used as a target level.

In August 1994, the JPPC released a discussion paper on a rate-based funding approach for Ontario public hospitals. The committee concluded that the limitations in the cost-based approach could be addressed using a "closed-ended" rate-based funding approach where patient volumes are negotiated between the Ministry of Health and hospitals. The formula seeks to integrate the currently diverse streams of hospital funding — global, inflationary, new program, growth, life support, equity, small hospital and special program funding — into one. This mix of funding streams is driven by different approaches:

Global-Historical: A hospital's budget allocation is based primarily on past funding allocations. The funding envelope is adjusted annually to reflect changes in input costs — goods and labour — changes in the volume and acuity of services provided, and changes in the total pool of funds available for hospitals.

Population-Based: Allocation of resources to different geographical areas is based on population size, age, gender mix and other characteristics. These specifics are used to assess the relative need for health services. Demands must be supported by population statistics.

Output-Based: Allocation is based on the volume and mix of services that an institution provides regardless of the size or make-up of the referral population. Funding may be related to actual costs incurred (cost-based), patient charges (charged-based) or on standard rates based on what the funding agent is willing to pay (rate-based). Output-based promotes efficiency, the higher a hospital's output and the lower its costs, the greater its financial gain.

Program-Based: Resources are earmarked for specific programs, enabling the Ministry to target and adjust funding on a program specific basis. This instills greater accountability for patient volumes and facilitates the identification and controlled introduction of new and emerging technologies into hospitals.(JPPC 1994)

The committee reviewed funding approaches across Canada and in other countries. Many jurisdictions were found to be incorporating an adjustment for case-mix in the funding of acute care hospitals. Diagnostic Related Groups (DRGs) or Case Mix Groups (CMGs) are being used to fund all or portions of hospital budgets. In the Ontario case, a fundamental shift was made when adjustments to funding started to incorporate hospital outputs — case-mix volumes — instead of relying solely on input cost data.

After extensive discussion, the committee decided in favour of a rate-based funding approach. Standard payment rates are established for the provision of standard patient services. A major consideration in the new direction was the impact of funding information feedback on hospital management. Rates create a conceptual shift in management responsibility, from the funder to the provider. A rate-based system forces hospitals to make tough management decisions, focusing more on defining their "product lines" and reducing their costs, and spending less time contesting reimbursement rates. Costs become more a management, and less a funding, issue. Hospitals will be preoccupied with *actual* input costs and not with what it *should* cost to provide a given service.

The new formula builds on an existing methodology — the Equity Funding Formula — which calculates an acute and newborn cost (ANBC) for each hospital. Using this ANBC and the number of weighted cases performed in the hospital, an average cost per weighted case is calculated. The Equity formula was founded on the principle that hospitals should receive comparable funding for comparable workloads. This principle was then applied to inpatient activity.

The Ministry of Health and various previous joint committees consistently recognized that the formula and the calculated cost per weighted case were not intended to represent comprehensive measures of hospital activity. The methodology has, historically, been endorsed to measure imbalances in acute inpatient care, the major component of hospital activity. Consequently, a calculated imbalance, above or below some level related to a funding imbalance for a hospital's acute inpatient care, irrespective of other activities, was accepted.

The JPPC's system of performance indicators appears to meet all necessary criteria. The Joint Policy and Programme Committee (JPPC) is itself a consensual body comprised of members of the Ministry of Health, local administrative heads, and professional and community representation. Information and report formats have been standardized across hospital information and accounting systems. And, a set of key criteria — standardized costs for pre-natal and acute care case-mix hospital peer groups — have been defined as the markers. The critical difference is that in Ontario, performance indicators are now being used directly to determine the level of transfer grants to local hospitals, at the heart of their operating revenues.

Though the system of performance indicators in place in the Ontario public hospital system was developed to assist in the allocation of incremental new resources (Warrian 1995), they now have become the lead instrument for administrative cuts and a market-type mechanism for hospital funding as a whole. In the Orwellian new system, rather than determining a funding allocation, a hospital's performance relative to its peers determines the relative funding cut it will sustain, between two and half per cent and seven and a half percent (2.5%-7.5%) in fiscal 1997, more in 1998.

Ontario has not moved to a formal purchaser-provider split or instituted a market-type mechanism for hospital funding. In the NHS case, professional observers have remarked that major changes in the organizational environment add a degree of bite to other developments. In particular, the purchaser-provider split increases the pressure to define and cost services, thereby making professional activities increasingly transparent to managers. In defiance of recent rhetorical conventions, the new Conservative Minister of Health in Ontario stated that you *do* have to be a rocket scientist to understand the new funding formula he has introduced. Perhaps. However, the impacts are quite straight forward. Cuts in operating grants will come by direct intervention, that is, they will be directly administered by the Ministry. Local hospital administration is then challenged to change their place in the queue through interaction with their local employee groups and bargaining agents. In the past, the union bargaining strategy was based on standardized labour costs. In future, hospitals will argue that they can't afford the general pattern because their costs and revenues are different. The weight of bargaining will have to be carried by union locals, not central office.

Patient-Centred Care (PCC)

Patient-centred care is a prime focus in reorganization of service delivery in Ontario hospitals. The objective is to move away from fragmented and "stove-pipe" approaches to patient services where, traditionally, patients were subject to a revolving door of interventions and shuffled physically between service areas within a hospital. Consultancy studies show overwhelming general and specific evidence of the waste in the present system as well as the potential cost and quality benefits of moving to alternative strategies and arrangements, such as PCC. Adopting PCC would re-group services so that an "expanded role nurse" will lead a team of service workers — formerly separate dietary, portering, laundry, nurses aides — as well as a technical team — pharmacy, laboratory, etc. — in integrated service delivery on the ward itself. Major cost savings would accrue from job combination — multi-skilling and multi-tasking — and from location of service teams on the wards themselves. And, in the expanded role, nurses would take over some diagnostic and medical duties from doctors.

The objective of patient-centred care is to reduce costs and improve quality. A typical example is the programme at University Hospital in London, Ontario, a 350-bed teaching hospital. In the past, an average acute care patient was admitted for four days, during which time they would interact with about sixty (60) different employees. Patients received state-of-the-art clinical care but at a high price and with a lack of continuity of care. Patient-centred care seeks to address the deficiencies of the system. A Hay Group study estimates that, on average, registered nurses spend only twenty-six per cent (26%) of their time in professional nursing including physical assessments, care and treatments, monitoring patients' conditions and planning and documenting care. The greatest portion of time — fifty-two per cent (52%) — is consumed in housekeeping details, answering phones and ordering supplies. To transform work practices, University Hospital's strategy calls for a substantial restructuring of nursing and allied health services within the hospital. The objective is a system with fewer nurses and fewer allied health professionals, but with greater opportunities to use their expertise in the care of patients, with better support and technical services to help them use their time appropriately. The strategy calls for development of multi-skilled service workers for support services and technological care, and reorganization of senior nurse clinicians into expanded roles. New job titles include patient services assistant, patient services technician and expanded role nurse:

- A **Patient Services Assistant** will combine and carry out tasks of housekeeper, dietary aide, porter and nursing assistant. Functions of the role will include, amongst others: orienting the patient to the nursing unit, handing out and picking up meal trays, feeding patients, answering the patient call system and responding to requests not requiring a nurse, making beds, cleaning patient rooms, checking supplies, ordering and putting away stock. These functions have traditionally been carried out by staff in separate classifications in the Environmental, Nutrition and Food, Materials Management, Property Services and Nursing Departments. The Patient Services Assistant will function under the direction of the bedside nurse or primary nurse. The primary nurse will perform the more complex aspects of nursing care such as assessment, planning, teaching, evaluation of care and specialized treatments and procedures.
- Functions of the **Patient Services Technician** will include phlebotomy, some physical therapy, respiratory therapy, EEG and anaesthesia procedures. In clinical areas such as emergency, the operating room and intensive care, new high-technology will allow primary nurses to delegate responsibility to the Patient Services Technician for highly specialized technical aspects of care.
- The **Expanded Role Nurses** are responsible for expert nursing care and basic medical management of patients in four areas: neurosurgery, cardiology, orthopaedics and renal dialysis. Some of the tasks traditionally within the territory of physicians are being transferred to Expanded Role Nurses, including daily health status assessments, application of basic medical knowledge, advance knowledge in the use of drug

therapies and awareness of appropriate manipulation of medications, interpreting basic x-ray films and more complex laboratory results; awareness of appropriate use of medical treatments according to diagnoses, and writing specific chart orders including treatments and medications in consultation with the physician.

The work and responsibility changes in the above description are relatively straight forward. The services technicians and assistants have broad new duties, and probably more challenging and better jobs. However, in labour-management terms it is a quagmire. About fifteen jobs are being combined across three bargaining units and four unions: SEIU, CUPE, ONA and OPSEU. There will be a net increase in jobs, but different jobs at the bottom and fewer at the top. In the typical case, SEIU and CUPE will gain members, OPSEU will lose in laboratories and ONA will lose nurses.

Sunnybrook Health Science Centre: A Model for Multi-Skilling

Toronto's Sunnybrook Health Science Centre is one of the largest hospitals in the country and among the most advanced in new employment relations and work organization for health care service delivery. To the extent that the health care and hospital sector has been the paradigmatic leader in shaping public sector labour-management relations over the past decade, Sunnybrook's innovations in multi-skilling offer an interesting case study for multi-skilling, not only in health care, but across the public sector.

At Sunnybrook, multi-skilling is seen as part of an overall restructuring plan for moving from traditional nursing units to patient-focused or patient-centred care. The new Sunnybrook multi-skilled service worker participates as a member of the patient care team and is responsible for the total environment of the patient. The stated purpose is to reverse the cumulative impact of multiple job classifications in the service area which differentiate jobs and fragment work processes. In the view of the administration, the productivity gains from multi-skilling are directly linked to reduction of these duplications and of time spent on stand-by or awaiting instructions. By designing job content and work flow more consistently and providing employees with a broadened skill base to accomplish multiple tasks, major inroads are made in reducing time spent on stand-by. Quality improvement is also addressed by reducing work process fragmentation. Multiple staff involvements during a single patient stay means accountability and responsibility for various tasks often slip between one employee classification and another. Patients recount incidents such as food trays delivered but left out of reach. The re-engineered system establishes responsibility and accountability on the part of the worker and minimizes slippage of tasks between job classifications.

The new, multi-skilled service assistants report to the manager of the patient unit. They are assigned a number of patients on the floor and are responsible for all environmental, dietary and transportation services required by those patients. During the course of their shift they may be assigned to maintain central areas such as patient lounges or utility rooms. Service assistants are scheduled from 7:30 a.m. to approximately 9:00 p.m. with a peak in numbers between 10:00 a.m. and 2:00 p.m., and work seven days a week on a rotating schedule.

This move to multi-skilling, with task flexibility and more fluid job definitions, represents a major break with traditional Wagnerism based, as it is, on job control unionism. Converting to multi-skilling at Sunnybrook began by a management-led process identifying broad skill areas relevant to the new service and corporate objectives:

- patient-centred care
- shared governance
- teamwork
- interaction skills with patients and families
- quality management
- customer service
- change management
- regulatory and legislative accountabilities

For each of these areas, knowledge, skills and attitude subsets were identified and a curriculum component developed. A joint union and management Multi-skilling Task Force designed the job description for the new service assistant position. Regular meetings

of the joint committee and focus groups of employees and supervisors were held over a period of approximately a year to come to agreement on a job description, role content, an educational program and a method of employee selection for the new positions. The new role included an amalgamation and redesign of all activities previously performed by seven classifications:
- Unit Aide
- Health Care Aide
- Dietary Aide
- Orderly
- Porter
- Housekeeper
- Attendant

Following this agreement, employee selection and compensation were negotiated by a joint labour-management Staff Planning Committee provided for under the local collective agreement with SEIU. The salaries of all seven job classifications were rolled into the service assistant position and were averaged to produce a new salary classification. Employees already earning beyond this amount were red circled and will not be given increases until their salary amount is in line with the classification. Those earning below the determined salary were brought up to the new salary scale. The union has grieved the final determination of the wage rate for the service assistant position.

Restructuring efforts such as multi-skilling are expensive on the front end, where costs include managers' time, paid education leave for the trainees, replacement of those performing their jobs while education is undertaken, training materials and increased equipment and supplies for the patient unit. At Sunnybrook there is no anticipated downsizing of front line service employees. Cost savings are not immediately realized, but are expected at the supervisory levels within the central departments as the number of service assistants under the supervision of the patient unit managers reaches a new level. It is no longer necessary to have separate supervisors and managers in dietary, laundry, portering and other areas.

At Sunnybrook, the promise of the new work organization theory is only partially being realized to date, which may validate union skepticism that new management re-engineering is simply a fad. An external evaluation by the University of Toronto Hospital Management Research Unit revealed the gaps between the rhetoric and the reality:

- significant variation in the degree to which service assistants receive regular communication, participate in decision-making, and perceive influence over decisions
- service assistants do not work in teams with nurses or other unit staff; work assignments are one contributing factor
- significant variation between types of care to the extent which service assistants work closely with nurses or with each other
- service assistants experience much less supervision than in previous jobs and are unclear about who supervises them
- service assistants receive little information about quality monitoring results
- strategies to systematically improve the quality of the service assistants' work do not exist.

The movement from the old paradigm to the new managerialism has clearly started, but the results to date are less than perfect. The impact on labour-management relations has been inconclusive. Consultants fees running into the millions of dollars have been spent to produce new re-engineering designs for hospitals, but most have been only partially implemented. The system is currently in stalemate for two reasons. The very procedure of business process re-engineering contains a fundamental contradiction. By design it is management-driven, but the implementation process must be from the bottom up. Employee groups *and* line supervisors both strongly resist BPR because they have largely been excluded from the process and don't believe their interests have been adequately incorporated. Inevitably, wholesale restructuring requires re-negotiation of collective agreements, but no one knows where or how that is to be done. The BPR consultants don't know and aren't trusted by the employee side. Management has felt hostage to centralized bargaining and therefore no proactive bargaining agenda for mutual gains bargaining exist. The system is in a stalemate.

Performance Indicators in Action: Redcliffe Hospital, Queensland, Australia

Redcliffe Hospital is a major teaching hospital in the Sunshine Coast Region of Queensland, Australia, which has built a reputation for effective management, high levels of staff commitment and a range of innovative practices, especially in its nursing division. Redcliffe also makes use of diverse clinical and operational indicators to measure performance against defined criteria.

The purpose of Redcliffe's Performance Indicator Project was to identify a more focused, organization-wide productivity scorecard for the hospital. This in turn would reflect their broad range of activities, set measurable performance goals and outcomes and enable staff and management to evaluate progress towards those goals. Another important aspect of the Project was that the scorecard would not be specific to Redcliffe. Rather, it would have wider application to other health care organizations as they moved towards hospital workplace restructuring and local bargaining agreements throughout the health sector in the state of Queensland.

Redcliffe's Productivity Scorecard

Customer Service Indicators
Goal: high quality patient care
Measures:
- patient survey and resolution of complaints
- patient incidents, mobility and education
- discharge planning and unplanned readmission rate
- hospital waiting lists & average waiting times

Internal Process Indicators
Goals: effective and efficient delivery of care
Measures:
- internal customer surveys
- medication errors and prescription problems
- infection rate and control

- audits of pain relief and pain service, cleaning service, catering and hotel service audit

Innovation and Learning Indicators
Goals: new skills, technologies and clinical practices
Measures:
- new skill acquisition, education and training programmes
- research output and budget
- introduction of new technologies and information systems
- introduction of new clinical models and practices

Financial Results Indicators
Goals: cost control and value for money
Measures:
- occupied bed days
- total admissions
- average inpatient cost per diagnostic related group
- throughput per bed

Workforce Role Indicators
Goals: caring, flexible and productive workforce
Measures:
- staff satisfaction survey
- absenteeism and unplanned roster changes
- staff participation in patient education, preceptor programmes, work reorganization
- implementation of key accountabilities
- job security and ratio of displaced persons redeployed
- staff support and counselling

Very broad performance indicators are being introduced in Canada and are being linked directly to the budget process. Performance-based budgeting is the new hammer in the system. Its impact will be felt most in local organizations. Central organizations — government, OHA and other employee associations and union head offices — will largely be on the sidelines. The only exception is B.C. where the government has decided it will try to soften the hammer's fall. The action will be local and complex. The simple world of bureaucrats and politicians will continue to spew out simplistic formulas. Local labour and management deal in the actualities, with patients, employees and the complex relations of different occupational, supervisory and patient groups. For these reasons the future in Canada is likely to look more like the Redcliffe model than like the JPPC at Sunnybrook.

The Failure of Conventional Productivity Measurement for Public Sector Services

The labour and management parties in Australia and elsewhere are trying to change their whole approach. The conventional approach to productivity measurement is based on narrow accounting definitions with little relevance to local hospital bargaining and workplace change. Accountants and traditional economists try to simply measure output per unit of input. For indicating performance in the public sector, conventional productivity measurement has fundamental defects:

- assumes a product of uniform quality, whereas most organizations, including health care, have multiple outputs and treat quality as a key ingredient of performance
- cannot shift to customer-driven, high quality products and processes based on technical specialists, segmented markets and service delivery
- relies on a "single factor" productivity ratio — such as tonnes of steel per employee per year — emphasizing reducing labour costs through job loss rather than improving the efficiency and effectiveness of the organization as a whole
- does not measure degree of workplace cooperation and involvement in company decisions about change; international experience of workplace productivity bargaining suggests the above strongly influences performance outcomes

- measures only past events, rather than addressing current operational performance trends; this in turn limits relevance for organizations whose strategy requires a tool not only for measuring performance but also for driving it.

Organizations need productivity measurement that lets them know what is happening now, in order to make decisions about the future. Public sector service needs a multi-factor approach, capable of measuring complex and qualitative outputs and outcomes.

Managerialism in Health Care: Promises, Realities and Labour-Management Relations

It has been suggested that the benefit of managerialism, particularly of the second wave, in Britain's NHS, is ambiguous. The newly emergent health consumerism and the potential for new managerial roles for professional employees will give the stakeholders greater say. The forced march of change in Ontario public health involves similar, though more compacted, potentialities.

In the NHS, the introduction and evolution of managerialism comprised three factors:
- direct intervention with the establishment of systems of general management and restrictions on the traditional role of professions and trade unions
- incorporation of professional groups through inclusion in new budgetary mechanisms and participation in quality improvement programmes
- and changes in the overall operating environment such as institutionalizing the purchaser-provider split and establishment of local trusts and service purchase agreements.

While developments in the NHS took place over the course of a decade, Ontario is witnessing the cascading, simultaneous introduction of all three forms so hastily that they reinforce each other and escalate the agenda of change. For instance, transfer payments have been linked directly to a case-mix peer performance indicator system — as discussed earlier — melding together the imposition of general management systems and changes in the overall environment. Patient-centred care has become a force-fed process of quality improvement at the same time that it is primarily represented as a means for cost-saving and competitive advantage within peer group hospitals. Currently, the nurses union and other bargaining agents are presented with aggressive proposals for job and duty consolidation and broad-banding. This is underway at a pace that allows little in scope for contributing professional judgements of the non-medical professional staff, let alone the non-professional service staff.

A recent study (for complete data see Appendix 1) examined collective agreement and workforce data from several hospitals in Ontario. Despite individual differences, it is possible to identify two basic patterns or trends, towards either a **traditional**, top down, rigid work rule environment, or a more **flexible** and less regimented example. These two ideal types were then used to simulate responses to a dramatic change in the fiscal environment for the hospital, not unlike the current actual experience in Ontario.

The traditional hospital goes into a downward spiral of layoffs, service cuts, more layoffs, more cuts. The more flexible multi-skilled hospital goes through a short-term budget shortfall, then recovers within three years. Though the simulation model is based on a hypothetical case and its purpose is to be a learning tool rather than as a predictive instrument, nonetheless, in summary terms, the results are reasonable approximations of the potential impacts on hospitals with different labour-management regimes faced with a twenty per cent (20%) transfer payment cut. To date, the Harris government has announced an eighteen per cent (18%) reduction across the board. More precise results could be obtained by further examination of individual hospital data and further refinement of the model.

The simulation indicates that however the potentialities of the emergent managerial system work out, the economic productivity gains to be realized through patient-centred care-type work reorganization strongly favour moving in this direction. But, the quality accomplishments suggested by the proponents of patient-centred care may take longer and are less evident. The impact of mechanically pegging transfer payments to cost-based case mix formulas like the JPPC performance indicators will mean that quantity improvements come first, quality later, if ever.

At the local hospital level, patient-centred care at present, appears to be a short-term fix for the fiscal pressure that is force-fed productivity improvement. All hospitals are to become like Toyota auto factories. If an industrial example of efficiency is to be used, GM's Saturn would be more appropriate, where the goal is long run improvement of quality and efficiency of health service delivery. Even giving the benefit of the doubt to proponents of patient-centred care, its positive potential is only realizable within the context of a fundamentally different model of management authority and a very different approach to labour-management relations.

As stated at the outset of this chapter, the health care sector has been the largest and leading case of broader public sector labour relations. It has been characterized, particularly over the past twenty years, by very large fiscal transfer payments, centralized collective bargaining and very standardized, traditional — read Wagnerist — approaches to wages, work rules and service delivery. This is all changing extremely quickly, under the forced march of budgetary pressures. Cost and performance improvements are now mandated by central governments. Yet there is no single "plan." Central bargainers are largely marginalized. The local change process is more often being driven by external consultants who have no answers beyond downsizing and contracting out. The focus will now shift to labour-management innovation in local and perhaps regional hospitals. New local agreements will have to be productivity-based. Redcliffe Hospital, Australia, provides a snapshot of this future. Trade unionists and hospital managers will either struggle toward some approximation of Redcliffe or they will lapse into a downward spiral of bloody-mindedness.

— CHAPTER 4 —
EVOLUTION OR DEVOLUTION?
Municipal Service Reform

In Canada, municipalities are often the front line of the public sector. Because of the immediate services municipalities provide — ploughing roads or fixing backed-up sewers — and the transparency of the property tax — municipal governments send property tax bills directly to taxpayers — monetary wage settlements in the municipal sector tend to attract closer public scrutiny. The phrase "government in a fish bowl" alludes to this high visibility of municipal councils and employees. For public sector labour-management relations this means ability to pay arguments, whether made by management or labour, are hotly contested. Current reductions in transfer payments will place extreme pressure on municipalities to cut services or raise taxes directly, or indirectly, through new user fees.

Municipal labour-management relations are among the oldest and most traditional in the public sector. They were somewhat overshadowed by developments in health and education in the 1970s and 1980s, but in the late 1990s, municipal labour-management relations again move to centre stage. Local managerialism, contracting out and the cost pressures-service delivery tradeoffs will be heavily felt at the municipal level because here all other budgetary programme cuts and immediate feedback from the public are most vividly apparent. This new pressure cooker of municipal labour-management relations and the more general issue of management by contract, instead of through traditional administrative and budgetary control systems, is well worth examining.

Municipal Labour-Management Relations: Bargaining in a Fish Bowl

Wage settlements for police and firefighters, whose salaries often amount to sixty per cent (60%) of municipal budgets, are most often the headline grabbers in media coverage of municipal labour-management relations. The progress of police and firefighter salaries, set through bargaining and arbitrating, displays some sense of the immediacy of bargaining at the local government level.

As relatively high-cost and labour-intensive departments, fire services have been the target of budget-cutters in municipal governments across the country for some years now, to a much greater extent than police services. In the "fish bowl" of local public service labour relations, budget-cutters know that demand for police and fire services have been evolving in opposite directions: while crime rates continue to rise, improvements in building codes, alarm and sprinkler systems have reduced the need for fire suppression.

Wage growth for police and firefighters tracked together, are well above general private and public sector wage patterns. The percentage increase from 1967 to 1985 for the average salaries of both groups was significantly greater than the percentage increase in the Consumer Price Index or in the Industrial Composite Average. Mean wages for police and firefighters changed by different percentages from year to year, but over the period from 1967 to 1985 they each increased — remarkably — by exactly the same proportion: 460.6%.

The bargaining position for both groups was intrinsically strong because their wages were, by almost any standard, extremely low in the mid-1960s. In a regime where the salary determination process turned on comparisons, it was easy to make a persuasive case. In this, police in particular were aided by the dramatic changes in their working conditions with the disturbing new social problems becoming apparent in the later 1960s — drugs, rising crime, demonstrations and confrontations with public authority. Again it was relatively easy to make a good case to an arbitrator that $6,300 per year was inadequate compensation for anyone confronted with the conditions faced on the streets by police officers. The firefighters, engaged in battle with the physical elements rather than with those confronting the law, were less dramatically affected by societal changes. But since they were seen to belong to the same category as the police, their wages remained linked, if not absolutely tied, to their colleagues.

Both groups have enjoyed other bargaining advantages. In those jurisdictions where the "employer" is a local police commission or a group of elected officials, most often with limited labour relations experience, police and firefighter associations have come to the bargaining table better prepared, with more experienced negotiators, and supplied with better data.

Police and firefighter associations share certain qualities which give them a unique character within the public and private sector collective bargaining system in Canada. Both sets of associations have served their members extremely effectively in the period since the mid-1960s, attaining significant control over many areas of members' work lives and increasing their real income more than that of virtually any other group in the labour force. By the 1990s, this was causing tension with other groups. Inside and outside workers, municipal office staff, social and health care workers in CUPE were facing huge pressures for contract concessions even though they had the same local employer. Meanwhile, employment relations for police and firefighters seemed to inhabit another universe.

Reduced Transfer Payments — A New Service Environment

Like other federal states, Canada has a well-developed system of intergovernmental transfer payments from federal to provincial levels, and from the provinces to local authorities and social agencies. Most public sector services are delivered at the local level by lower tier organizations such as municipal governments, school boards, hospitals and social agencies. Most public expenditure actually occurs at this level, and directing these activities is the principal function of Canadian public sector management.

The system is facing major changes in transfers from the federal government to the provinces and in turn, to local authorities, for expenditures in health, education and welfare. In its February, 1995 budget, the federal government announced its intention to substantially reduce its funding of health, education and welfare. (Canada 1995) The funds involved are the largest single items in Canadian government budgets.

Federal Transfer Payments to Provinces
for Health, Education & Welfare
1993-1998
(Millions of Dollars)

1993-94	1994-95	1995-96	1996-97	1997-98
28,955	29,428	29,686	26,900	25,100

In addition, the federal government is changing to a system of block funding. The proposal is to consolidate these separate streams into a new Canada Health and Social Transfer (CHST). The change is rationalized on the basis that it will allow those delivering services to manage the system in new, more flexible and effective ways. Provinces will no longer be subject to rules stipulating conditions for program delivery in cost-shared expenditures and will be free to pursue their own innovations in social security reform. In turn, federal expenditures will no longer be driven by provincial decisions on how, and to whom, to provide social assistance and social services.

With regard to national service standards in this changing environment, the same federal budget proposed requirements that focus primarily on the traditional eligibility criteria of accessibility, affordability and public administration for health services and secondarily on prohibition of minimum residency requirements for social assistance entitlement. The on-going official federal-provincial discussions on block funding remain focused on the input side, rather than on outputs or outcomes. If discussion of the change is frozen at this level, then the move to block funding will remain trapped in traditional approaches to public sector management. Were that to remain the case, there would be minimum impacts on labour relations. In fact, the world is changing far more than that.

The "off-loading" from one level of government to another provides the major trigger for re-conceptualization of the role for each level in the transfer chain. Long-term financial, service delivery and policy issues are now emerging that align closely with international developments associated with a new and different economic theory applied to the public sector: the formulations and predictions of principal-agent theory.

Service Reform Trends Internationally

Three trends in reform of public sector service delivery have been identified in New Zealand, the United Kingdom, Australia and Canada, with similar constitutional and budgetary systems:

- **corporate management**, direct provision by government departments
- **service agreements or contracts** between separate funding authorities and agencies — public, community or private — responsible for service delivery
- **contracting out**, competition and competitive tendering for contracts for public service delivery (McGuire 1994)

The fundamental differences in these three approaches are in the separation of policy formulation and service delivery, the use of program budgeting or contracts and the extent of competition between providers to manage service delivery. New Zealand and the UK have introduced market competition for public service delivery. In contrast, Canadian and Australian national governments have, until recently, relied upon corporate management, program budgeting and evaluation. These new reforms tie public service funding to specified performance indicators.

To date, Canadian federal public management reform has relied upon corporate management within the public sector to improve efficiency and effectiveness of service delivery. The objective of the federal *Public Service 2000* initiative, introduced in 1989, was to make the costs of service provision transparent to ministers, as well as the public. Departments were required to develop service standards in consultation with clients and publish these in the budget papers. There has been explicit emphasis on accountability and cost-cutting. Standards have been based on the costs of providing service rather than quality. Again, service standards are seen as a means of reducing the costs of service delivery and thereby the budget deficit. (Weller et al 1993; Spice 1993)

By contrast, under the Australian Financial Management Improvement Program (FMIP), government departments and agencies are required to set measurable objectives for programs and evaluate performance on the basis of these measures. The problems with this model are a lack of devolution of financial and staffing control to program managers and inadequate development of performance indicators. (Stewart & Walsh 1993; Howard 1991)

In New Zealand and the U.K., experience with management by contracts has given chief executives of agencies much greater control over resource allocation within their organizations. These contracts create trading relations between ministries and/or departments — who decide what is to be provided — and the agencies contracted to provide specific services. Government priorities are reflected in the total budget allocations. Departments and agencies are then responsible for the outputs of their organizations. Wherever possible, a single public service provider has been replaced by competition between providers, and demand is managed on a user-pay basis. The emphasis is changing to direct exchange of services between the public and agencies. However, in health and education services in both the UK and New Zealand, central agencies, rather than direct payment by parents and patients, determine resource allocation. Competition is for funding rather than for consumers with schools and hospitals competing against each other for budget resources. (McGuire 1994)

Recent developments indicate that the Canadian federal government is moving away from corporate management of direct delivery of social programmes, vacating the field to the provinces. The local, front-line level of government and agencies are bearing the greatest burden of adjustment to these changes reflected in the federal government's downsizing of 45,000 employees and transfer of jurisdiction to the provinces. At the level of municipal government and other social agencies, developments may well proceed towards a combination of service and contract agreements, moving the system in the direction of contractualism. For labour-management relations this means a very different direction and form of negotiation. For example, wage and work rule provisions in contracts, and even entire contracts, will be dependent on securing and keeping service provision agreements with other levels of government. In the Ontario government's "workfare" program, for instance, funding will depend on as yet unspecified performance measures.

Contracting Out: Theory vs. Practice

Throughout the 1980s, contracting out of services, particularly garbage collection and transportation, was one of the most contentious labour-management issues in the municipal field. In the late 1990s, it threatens to become a generalized phenomenon across the country, across all sectors.

Ironically, at the very time that contracting out has come to be perceived by local management as a catch-all relief from budget pressures, the mounting longitudinal evidence shows this phenomenon creates its own large net costs. In the long run, there may be more economic advantage to improving current public sector practices from within. There is no evidence favouring blanket acceptance of contracting out.

Why is contracting out not necessarily less costly than *efficient* government operations, where efficiency is measured in the total costs of each unit of service provided? Contingent contracts and opportunistic behaviour of private firms cause significant contracting costs in the form of monitoring outlays. Studies estimate that total contracting costs — contract letting, administration and monitoring — range from a low of four point four per cent (4.4%) of total costs to a high of thirty-three per cent (33%). To be clear, these are expenses *in addition* to the direct costs of service delivery.

American data covering the last decade yields the following examples of administrative add-on costs of contracting out as a percentage of total costs:

Street Cleaning	11.9%	Janitorial	34.9%
Refuse Collection	4.4	Payroll Preparation	68.7
Traffic Signals	18.1	Road maintenance	5.0
Lawns	33.1	Street trees	25.7

While there is abundant evidence *purporting* to demonstrate the cost-effectiveness of contracting out, there is no convincing proof that it actually reduces costs. In fact, it can be more costly. In New Jersey, where the neo-conservative government and Governor have been much heralded by the new Conservative government in Ontario, approximately half of contracted-out municipal services have resulted in "unreasonable cost increases" according to local municipal officials. (Prager, 1994)

Management agreements at the bargaining table are entirely restricted to debates over the direct costs of service and omit these additional monitoring costs, which are substantial. It usually comes down to union versus non-union wage rates. A cynic would argue that while there is little evidence that contracting out works, there is abundant evidence that the *threat of contracting out works*, if it moves the parties to jointly seek new arrangements to reduce costs and improve services *within* the public sector. In the near term, CUPE will overwhelmingly bear the brunt of contracting out pressure at the municipal level. After a lag, the same pressure will be felt on police and firefighters.

At the root of the contracting issue is an entirely new aspect of public administration that has previously been ignored – the principal-agent problem. To the extent that contracting becomes more pervasive in the public sector, "agency costs" will take on a central importance in the new public sector economic paradigm.

Principal-Agent Theory and Federal States

In the principal-agent model, the agent makes decisions on behalf of the principal, for which the principal compensates the agent with payment or reward. An asymmetry of information and an implicit tension — if not conflict of interest — is assumed between the two parties. The principal cannot observe all the agent is doing, leaving the agent opportunity for discretionary behaviour. The principal cannot ensure the agent will make decisions optimal to the principal without incurring costs.

Agency costs have been calculated as:
- **monitoring costs:**
    expenditures the principal makes to limit activities of the agent that diverge from the principal's interest,

including direct supervision, budget restrictions, compensation policies, operating rules

- **bonding costs:**
  expenditures the agent makes to guarantee that his/her actions will not harm the principal or to compensate for harm

- **residual loss:**
  net income foregone by the principal due to the divergence between the agent's decisions and decisions which would maximize the net income of the principal.

To accomplish public policy objectives, public organizations must retain involvement in the decision-making of their agents for their organizations. Large, complex organizations confront sequences of principal-agent problems, from senior management to lower supervisors and employees, and with external contracting entities. Additional layers of complexity arise when dealing with inter-agency or inter-governmental arrangements accountable to different political authorities and holding competing policy objectives.

In federal states, the principal-agent issue arises where different levels of government share co-responsibility for finances, policy or a mix of the two. Relations between senior levels of government are typically governed by formal multi-year administrative agreements which define financial liabilities, general policy objectives, rules of eligibility and reporting requirements. Service delivery is usually in the hands of subsidiary units. How efficiently and effectively the program is managed and delivered effects the net financial obligations of the senior level of government. (Alford & O'Neill 1994; Moe 1984; Donaldson 1990; Marsden & Momigliano 1995)

Ontario's Municipal Support Program: A Test Site for NPM

Recent developments suggest that Mike Harris' Ontario government has chosen the municipal sector as a major experimentation site for the new public management. One of the least examined sections of the contentious 1996 Omnibus Bill-26 is "Appendix M" relating to municipalities. "Appendix M" provides a new framework for local managerialism. Policy-based targeted and conditional grants are replaced by a new block funding mechanism in the form of the Municipal Support Program (MSP) which gives local municipalities a much freer hand with much reduced — decreased by forty-seven per cent (47%) in the 1995-96 budget — provincial transfer grants. In addition, there is an exemption from the previous regime of provincial regulation on engineering standards, land use and other areas.

The Omnibus Bill also provides for the introduction of new standards for municipal service delivery through changes to audit standards. The provincial Ministry of Municipal Affairs has borrowed the tactic of John Major and his Citizens Charters, importing the parallel framework from the U.K. Audit Commission for Local Authorities (see Appendix 3). The Audit Commission Citizen's Charter Indicators are performance indicators that local authorities, the British form of local government, must apply to the services they provide. The Audit Commission compares levels of performance between local authorities in preparation for a national report. To encourage public involvement, the Commission presents questions for each of their performance indicators and requires authorities to publish their results in local papers. The Commission has stated that the public needs to receive comparativeness information during the reorganization of local government, so that a baseline is established against which public and local authorities themselves can assess the performance of any new local authorities.

The cumulative impact of these system changes is dramatic. Local officials, instead of interfacing with officials at the next level of government, must now face their local customer-citizens. The impact on labour relations will be two-fold. Broad comparisons — pattern bargaining — to other municipalities will become at best equal, if not secondary, to other productivity and performance measures. And, internal budget allocations will inevitably be related to price-performance criteria.

Municipal Planning for Performance: Sunneyvale, California

A leading example of how to do it right at the municipal level comes from Sunneyvale, California. For Canadian public managers Sunneyvale, California may be what Toyota was to GM fifteen years ago. President Clinton's 1993 *Government Performance and Results Act* was directly inspired by the comprehensive performance management and budgeting system developed by Sunneyvale, California. The federal Office of Management and Budget has testified that the city's system was the country's best example of performance measurement. Sunneyvale provides better services for lower taxes than similar municipalities, and with fifty-five per cent (55%) to sixty-five per cent (65%) fewer employees and pays city employees comparably higher wages.

Planning is long term, begins at the top and moves down the organization. The twenty-year General Plan consists of seven elements: transportation, community development, environmental management, public safety, socio-economics, culture, and planning and management. Each sets out goals, policies, and actions. The plans also provide the Community Condition Indicators, such as library visits per capita, which provide an objective basis for assessing progress towards goals. Every five years, Sunneyvale updates the General Plan, working with the public.

Budget planning is based on the ten-year Resource Allocation Plan, updated annually. This helps determine whether programs can be sustained in the long-term and assists the city to avoid unexpected fiscal shortfalls. While the figures for a decade may not be firm when first developed, annual revisions gradually move them toward actual expenditures. Sunneyvale does not project intergovernmental transfers beyond their guaranteed time-frame. Programs that depend on these transfers must show alternative sources of funding or be terminated.

The key planning device is the two-year Performance Budget, linked to the ten and twenty-year strategic plans. The Performance

Budget is organized by General Plan element rather than department. Departments focus on meeting the city's general goals rather than on internal departmental priorities. The two-year plan funds *tasks* rather than line-items. A unit cost is developed for each task assigned to city workers and is comparable throughout the municipality's operations. Rather than budget dollars, managers budget working hours necessary to achieve the unit requirements. The use of these units over time provides the measurable standard against which performance is judged. Rents and depreciation charges are also levied for all facility and equipment use.

Managers are assessed based on their success or failure in meeting plan objectives. Their wages are set by comparison to comparable municipalities and can vary as much as fifteen per cent (15%) based on performance. Every four weeks, program managers review management information reports that track municipal work and progress towards plan goals. The main incentive for managers is to achieve, or surpass, specified levels of service. This controls service levels and can free up money for other priorities. The overall performance of the city is summarized in the Annual Performance Report, shared with the public.

Re-engineering Service Delivery: Metro Toronto Social Services Division

Nowhere is the challenge to change municipal services to meet new performance and policy environments more difficult than in the welfare system.

At the provincial to municipal level of transfer, costs and benefits are shared across various entitlement programmes. The primary income support programme is General Welfare Assistance (GWA). Delivery is the responsibility of municipal governments such as Metropolitan Toronto, while policy definition and funding is jointly shared with the provincial government. The financial responsibility is shared eighty per cent (80%) provincial; twenty per cent (20%) municipal, with some variation by case type. Administrative costs are shared equally between province and municipality for all case types.

Program Cost Sharing
by Case Type

Case Type	Provincial Share	Municipal Share
Unable to Obtain Employment	80%	20%
Single Parent Families	100%	-
Short Term Illness	80%	20%
Long Term Illness	80%	20%
Students	80%	20%
Other	80%	20%

Problems with chronic, high unemployment have placed huge burdens on local social service delivery agents across Canada, none more so than in Metropolitan Toronto. It is the largest of Canada's cities and has the largest concentration of the unemployed and social assistance recipients. A tripling of the provincial unemployment level over five years (1989-1994) created what can only be described as a crisis in the welfare system. The General Welfare Assistance caseload tripled, averaging 121,500 cases per month in 1994, compared with 39,000 cases in 1989.

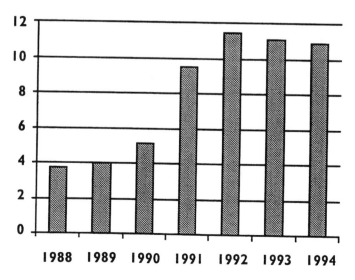

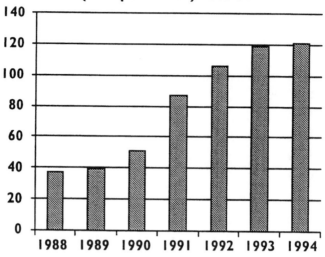

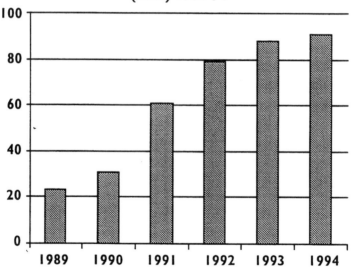

In 1994, more employable people than ever were on welfare. Seventy-three per cent (73%) of the overall caseload, an average of 92,000, were unemployed employable cases, compared with fifty-five per cent (55%) of the caseload, or 23,000, in 1989. In addition, people on welfare are having more difficulty than ever getting off. The average length of time on social assistance more than doubled, from less than six months in 1989 to sixteen months in 1994.

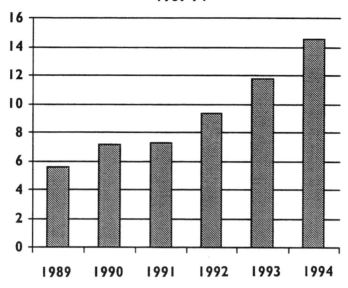

These economic and social circumstances placed unprecedented demands on the delivery of services. In the five-year period the case-to-worker ratio increased twenty-five per cent (25%) and the number of mandatory contacts by a caseworker increased by forty (40%). The number of individuals per caseworker increased by almost fifty per cent (50%). The annual programme dollars administered per caseworker doubled from $550,000 in 1989 to $1.1 million in 1994.

In response to the huge growth in the caseload and the demands on staff, the Metro Toronto Social Services Division embarked on an ambitious re-engineering of the service delivery system. The objectives were improved efficiency of administration and delivery, and better outcomes for social assistance recipients.

The overall objective of the re-engineering effort is to shift from traditional objectives of benefit administration and compliance to pro-active facilitation of clients into re-training, career development and job placement. Caseworkers have become the single access point for the complete range of benefits and services, spending an increasing portion of their time on client action plan development for re-entry into the labour market and to achieve economic self-sufficiency. New information technology — electronic fund transfer, automated information kiosks — has been introduced to reduce time-consuming manual administrative tasks. New partnerships were established with other community-based agencies for client support, job search, employment and training referrals. In light of the reduced administrative burden and availability of new technology, service standards were changed to raise the staffing ratios from one caseworker to 100 to one for each 120 clients. Service areas were reduced in number and front-line supervisory positions were reduced by twenty-five per cent (25%) with a change in the ratio of supervisors to caseworkers from one to seven to one to ten. (Metro Social Services 1995)

As noted elsewhere, information technology (IT) is a keystone of the business process that results from a re-engineering effort. (Halachmi 1995) IT forms a critical part of the new delivery system by bringing access to organizational databases closer to front-line service delivery personnel. Metro Social Services has made large commitments to developing a new Caseload Management Automation System to provide a wide range of client and management information to end-users by automating many processes. Initial pilots of the system have produced impressive results. Waiting time for in-office client interviews was reduced by twenty-one per cent (21%); replacing lost or stolen cheques takes one-third less time; screening and scheduling time for initial applications was reduced by sixty-nine (69%); detecting potentially fraudulent cases has been enhanced by one case per work day. (Municipality of Metropolitan Toronto 1995)

Caseworkers and other non-supervisory employees are represented by CUPE. Management of the Social Services Division negotiated formal adjustments to the collective agreement to facilitate the changes in policy and service direction, most important of which was a change in title for front-line staff to "caseworker" from the traditional "welfare visitor." While major progress has taken place in policy objectives, information technology and task definition for caseworker employees, aside from some adjustment in job titles and local flexibility in working conditions, the overall system of employee compensation remains unchanged, and very traditional. The central labour agreement is still framed in terms of rate-for-the-job and length-of-service pay increments. It has not matched developments in other OECD countries in moving public sector compensation towards an emphasis on pay-for-performance.(Marsden & Momigliano 1995)

In principal-agent terms, the above developments can be summarized as both the province and the municipality seeking to reduce their residual losses or costs by decreasing the duration of claimants and payment of benefits. The province, as principal, has an interest in more effective monitoring resources because, while general entitlement criteria have been established in legislation, regulations and administrative guidelines, the actual determination of entitlement and on-going monitoring of client behaviour is done by social workers employed by the municipality. In cost-shared programmes, the municipality also has an interest as a principal in limiting its residual losses with respect to the behaviour of its social worker employees and clients. The municipality has extended its expenditure of resources on bonding costs through re-negotiating its labour contract and engaging the clients in more pro-active labour market actions. The latter are expected to reduce the long-range residual losses for both the province and the municipality through better labour market outcomes.

To complement the re-engineering of service delivery, management of the Social Services Division has been seeking to define appropriate performance measurements and standards for assessing outcomes of service delivery. In the process of trying to develop metrics and standards, fundamental issues related to principal-agent and competing policy objectives have emerged.

Until the welfare reform movement of the later 1980s, the primary tasks of welfare staff were to process public assistance applications, determine eligibility, calculate grant amounts, assure timely delivery of benefits, and safeguard against fraud and abuse. (AWPA 1994) During the 1980s emphasis changed to more active labour-market focus and different measures have emerged to assess the effectiveness of programme delivery. The following client-based outcome measures have been deemed appropriate for managers of re-employment focused social assistance funding in the United States.

APWA Performance Standards

Policy Objective	Performance Objective	Metric
• Job Placements	• Post-secondary degree	• Target group diploma; GED
• Job Retention	• Completion of educational activity; improved competency	• Average time on benefits
• Wages/earnings at termination of JOBS	• Completion of job skills activity	• Number or percentage returning to benefits
• Employer health benefits	• JOBS participation; target group expenditures	• Number of single parents receiving child support
• AFDC case closed; grant reduced by earnings	• Target group enrolment	• Average cost per participant
• High school diploma; GED	• Target group placement, job retention	• Average cost per job placement

The APWA study on performance standards represents the leading edge in developing metrics which can assess fundamental issues of public service delivery. It seeks to provide a set of new management tools that will help overcome efficiency and effectiveness issues described by principal-agent theory. However, the process of developing these tools has itself identified incongruities in overall policy objectives with different outputs and outcomes. For instance, is the underlying policy objective of the welfare system to provide for minimum basic need, to punish those not working, or to facilitate long-term economic self-sufficiency through training, daycare and proactive employment services?

Measuring Performance in Social Services: Department of Adult and Family Services, Oregon

Since 1990, Oregon has published its biennial reports called "Oregon Benchmarks" which set broad social goals for state and local government. Like other government departments, the Department of Adult and Family Services (AFS) drafts mission statements, goals, values, and performance measures related to the Oregon Benchmarks and reports on a biennial basis. AFS performance measures include:
- percentage of teen parents in school
- percentage of departmental clients who complete employment and training programs
- average increase in grade level of clients.

These three measures support the "Urgent Oregon Benchmark" to give high school graduates the skills essential for success in life. The AFS mission is to help families become self-supporting while assisting them in meeting their basic needs. It is attempting to do this by measuring outcomes — client self-sufficiency, accurate and timely benefits, and labour force efficiency and diversity — rather than internal processes.

The department has been significantly restructured, hierarchies have been flattened, new technologies developed, divisional goals and performance measures established. Management has consciously sought to involve the appropriate union officials throughout. From 1993-95, AFS results include:
- a seven per cent (7%) decline in welfare caseloads
- cost-per-work placement falling from $4,200 to $2,165

- a higher proportion eighty-nine per cent (89%) of welfare teens are in school or have graduated than in any other state.

This success is supported by a comprehensive public- and private-sector partnership to subsidize and offer minimum wage job opportunities with local companies.

Metro Toronto, like other governments, is only now starting to confront measurement issues in the later stages of the re-engineering process rather than, as would be ideal, at the beginning. The interest of the province (as principal) is in limiting its funding liabilities in terms of the aggregate costs of social assistance benefits and the duration of claims. The province stipulates formal entitlement criteria which are then left to the agent — the administrators and staff of the Municipality of Metropolitan Toronto — to deal with assessment and eligibility decisions with the actual claimant. Metro Toronto has its own policy goals, in this case, the long-range self-sufficiency and labour market success of the claimants, particularly as the number of traditionally unemployables has grown. For this group, labour market success and self-sufficiency means major re-skilling and retraining for new occupations. This requires longer periods on benefits and the supply of new active labour market services. The result is a major increase in costs of benefits and services.

Differences in political philosophy can confound efforts at performance measurement and improvement. The Conservative Ontario government, which came to power in 1995 with different policy objectives, resolved its residual losses problem by unilaterally lowering the benefit level by twenty-three per cent (23%). Between 1992 and 1994 the Municipality of Metropolitan Toronto sought to improve outcomes by increasing its bonding costs with respect to the clients through "case management" techniques and re-organization of employees job duties towards more active labour market policies. This was a move away from the traditional "welfare visit" or enforcement cost approach, which emphasized compliance. Since 1995, the new provincial government is again emphasizing compliance, insisting on greater enforcement activities of staff and causing a reversion to higher enforcement costs. What is the real priority or objective?

The general movement towards decentralization in public service delivery and administration, along with constrained resources, appear to be the defining characteristics of public sector management in the coming years. The application of principal-agent theory to public administration has sought to import developments in the economics of organization, particularly the role of hierarchies, to identify areas of potential gain in efficiency and service delivery. All public sector service delivery organizations can benefit from the results of such analyses. In the case of Canada, and perhaps other federal states, inter-governmental arrangements constitute an environment in which principal-agent theory takes on additional and sometimes counter-intuitive aspects.

Recent dramatic changes have led to increased financial burden on all levels of government, resulting in efforts to reduce expenditures and improve outcomes in all programmes, including social assistance. This has caused governments to re-examine their financial and administrative arrangements. The huge increase in social assistance caseloads caused managers of service delivery to re-examine their efforts with respect to both workloads on social workers and outcomes for clients. With current labour market conditions, clients are not able to move off welfare into employment in the manner that they have historically. Re-engineering efforts at the delivery end, from the ground up, including the search for appropriate performance measures, revealed ambiguity and tension in overall policy objectives. These are driven in turn by fundamental principal-agent issues at the inter-governmental level. As the system seeks to manage these problems, it is predicted that forms of a contract state arrangement will emerge at the provincial-municipal level within the Canadian federal state.

Evolution or Devolution?
From Principal Agent Theory to the Contract State

Principal-agent theory has been most aggressively applied to public sector management in the UK, Australia and New Zealand. It has not been used between traditionally separate entities such as shareholders and managers, or management and employees, but applied to core operations of government. This has led to a new theory of the state itself — the Contract State — in which activity previously subject to organizational hierarchy is now governed by contracts, or quasi-contracts, between buyers and sellers, either inside or outside the public sector.

For academics, the Contract State is the logical conclusion of principal-agent theory. The Contract State is framed by five policy principles which flow from the notions of establishing contractual relationships between purchasers and providers, rigorously specifying the outputs to be provided and structuring clear incentives for providers to perform. They are:
- clear responsibility and accountability for results
- empowering consumers
- minimizing government bureaucracy
- preference for market mechanisms
- professional and business-like management of public agencies.

(Alford & O'Neill 1994)

The New Paradigm and Municipal Labour-Management Relations

Labour-management relations at the municipal level date back to the 1920s. They existed alongside the mass production private sector unionism that emerged in the 1930s and 1940s. As such, municipal labour-management has most closely followed the industrial model. Traditional approaches to contracts mean that job classifications and seniority rules at the municipal level are even more strongly weighted toward traditional hierarchy and rigidity than other parts of the public sector. (Rose 1996) This traditionalism in contracts has also existed alongside the direct and rigid feedback system of local media, municipal hothouse politics and ratepayer pressures. The intensity of the clash between traditional labour contract work rules and the 1990s fiscal and service performance improvement pressures will be most keenly felt at the local level. Contracting out will continue to appear as an easy and cost-efficient way to deal with budget pressures and taxpayer resistance, even if the real facts are otherwise. For all these reasons, the key test of public sector labour-management relations may come in the municipal sector.

Off-loading between levels of government, particularly between provincial and local levels, will come with strings attached. The new audit and service standards in Ontario and Alberta will serve as benchmarks. Even where funds are cutback, performance measures will still be introduced. Municipal taxpayers will also want clearer measures of how their tax dollars are being spent. Principal-agent theory may appear obtuse, but it gives practical insight into the direction and tensions of future developments. What this means for labour contracts is more contingent provisions; contingent on funding, performance and flexible delivery systems.

At the municipal level existing collective bargaining agreements have been overwhelmingly framed around the mass production — Wagner — model of standardized labour inputs and processes. While much of the new public sector management is striving towards the Toyota model — a system of relentless cost and quality improvement — arguably a more appropriate model for most public sector delivery is Saturn which better matches employee interest and service delivery. In any case, unions and managers who try to stick with the Wagner mass production model will face a future of chronic pressure to privatize and contract out. In that model, it was axiomatic that more or better service meant more money. If services can be sustained, let alone improved, with fixed or declining resources, then for political decision-makers the temptation will be a relentless political exit, cancelling services or giving them over to the private sector.

Conversely, for management, to simply resort to pervasive contracting out will mean long-term morale and productivity issues. The lessons of the private sector are clear, contracting everything out means putting yourself out of business — employees, managers and the organization itself. Public sector organizations will need to learn to manage the supply chain of their services and the economic value chain with a long term value and productivity goal of community service needs, just like the best of the private sector survivors.

Unions must be involved in workplace change, especially in public service, the most highly unionized sector of the national economy. Studies show that only those workplace innovations that combine substantial employee participation with the sharing of economic rewards raise productivity in private sector work places. Research also indicates that workplace innovations and employee-employer partnerships are more likely to produce productivity and service improvements in unionized settings. A study of employee involvement programs in one thousand union and non-union machine tool shops showed unionized firms gained greater worker control, enhanced job security, and significant productivity increases. In marked comparison, non-union firms' employee involvement programs resulted in less job security and job control and produced thirty to sixty-two per cent (30-62%) *less* in productivity. A direct translation of these results to the public sector is impossible. Research and measurement of the parallel development is necessary.

While Canadian examples are only beginning to emerge, unions and management in some American cities have begun to adjust to the changing public sector paradigm.

Contracting Out in Indianapolis: Civic Employees Bid for their Jobs

Municipal public service workers in Indianapolis, Indiana faced an incoming mayor elected on a promise to reduce the size of government by twenty-five per cent (25%). Police and fire services had been excluded from the pledge, and the local union realized half its membership was at risk. The new mayor quickly closed the maintenance garage, though no concrete data existed on whether the private sector could really do the job better. The union worked to foster a positive relationship with the mayor, encouraging him not to privatize for its own sake, but to concentrate on ensuring public services remain competitive.

The new transportation director, working with the union, developed an activity-based cost analysis intended to measure all costs associated with service delivery. The union was fully involved in the bidding process from the outset and won inclusion of legal, monitoring, and general management overhead in all bids. The burden of public sector overhead was reduced by the mayor's elimination of a significant number of management positions. The union researched new equipment, services routes, and redeploying resources. It negotiated new contract language requiring worker training before bids were released for competition and ensured lay-offs could not occur during the bidding process. The union also ensured that contractor's failures would be the contractor's responsibility and won tightened safety provisions.

Seventy-five per cent (75%) of all bids for city services have been won by the union. Under pressure for contracting out, the union became fully involved in change. Some work has been lost, but workers have become more flexible and accountable to their jobs. Workers have made the adjustment from traditional work styles to multi-skilling and broad-banded classification systems. Full union involvement in the process of change has meant that its successes have been highly publicized, countering common sense misconceptions of public service workers as not accomplishing productive work and of the private sector as inherently more efficient.

Canadian municipal unions may very well have to think the unthinkable and start making proposals on how they will participate in contracting out systems. A clear precedent is the Steelworkers achievement in monitoring and assembling bids for contracted work in the steel mills. If municipal unions try to retain the status quo, the dare will be thrown to management to proceed without them.

For the rest of the 1990s, no one in the municipal sector — not labour representatives nor management bargainers — will have the luxury of a no-change position. Labour-management relations will be transformed or they will be exited.

— CHAPTER 5 —
ONTARIO HYDRO:
Toward Participatory Change

For a pure case of fully developed public sector Wagnerism, one need look no further than labour-management relations at Ontario Hydro. Ontario Hydro is one of the largest utilities in the world, providing electricity from fossil fuel, hydro electric and nuclear power plants. Downward trends in energy prices over the years, combined with greater energy efficiency, have resulted in decreased demand for energy. Approaching the millennium, Ontario Hydro faces increasing pressure to privatize, in whole or in part. How long will taxpayers continue to foot the bill for a Crown corporation the size of Ontario Hydro? Can restructuring prevent full-scale privatization? These and other factors have prompted restructuring of the massive utility, and attempts to develop participatory labour-management relations in the change process.

From the beginning of electrical industry regulation in the early 1900s until recent decades, incremental technological advances in standard turbine, generator and transmission technologies provided economies of scale and decreasing unit costs. The regulatory regime for the industry was seen by most as oversight of a natural monopoly. This was validated by real costs and rates falling continually. (Hirsh 1990) Not surprisingly, the labour and management parties at Hydro adopted the same adversarial industrial relations practices — the Wagner model — as in other mass production industries characterized by standardized costs and economies of scale.

In the 1990s, the regulatory, financial and operational environment shifted. Ontario Hydro embarked on a major re-organization to meet the challenges of this new environment, restructuring into the following autonomous business units:

Upstream:	Nuclear	Fossil	Hydro Electric
Downstream:	Grid	Retail	Energy Services

What has yet to happen is a fundamental change in how labour and management do their business at Ontario Hydro. Various initiatives, discussed below, have been used in the past decade, but, until very recently, all have been within the existing structure. The industrial relations model at Hydro is in need of fundamental overhaul on both sides. Without it, the system will drift toward crisis.

Employees, Bargaining Units and Bargaining Agents

There are two unions at Ontario Hydro operations. The Power Workers' Union (PWU) has 15,000 members out of a current workforce of 22,000 and the Society of Ontario Hydro Professional and Administrative Employees (referred to as the Society) has 5,000 members. In addition, there are some 2,000 non-bargaining unit employees.

The typical PWU member is a technician with a high school education and eight to ten years training on the job. PWU members are very highly skilled but with very narrow firm-specific skills. There is relatively little mobility across business units, particularly in the upstream business units with heavy operational requirements. Workers in downstream business units possess more customer service and standardized skills.

The employment relations model is that of the traditional "tradesman." Employees enter through a regular apprenticeship or its five-year training equivalent, and stay in their entry slot more or less throughout their careers. Some sixty per cent (60%) of PWU members have trade certification, including the power line maintainers. The remainder are clerical and technical workers. The tradeworkers and operators progress through fixed job ladders. Clerical workers must apply for specific job openings. Technicians enter with their diplomas and stay in their occupational group.

The Society was given voluntary recognition by Hydro management in 1993. In contrast to the PWU, it is mostly comprised of university-educated professional engineers and technicians.

The Costs of Transformation

In recent years the relationship between Hydro management and the PWU has undergone cycles of cooperation and confrontation. Major conflicts over Hydro restructuring go back over a decade to Article 11 in the 1984 contract, concerning re-deployment. The complexities of the system embodied in Article 11 equal or exceed any parallel provisions in large private sector agreements. Its surplus staff procedure takes up eighteen full pages of the collective agreement, with twenty-seven official sub-clauses. (Hydro-PWU 1994) An indication of the elaborate detail of the provision is evident in section 11.1 which deals only with definitions and contains separate legal definitions for all of the following:

Classification	Occupational Group	Job Family
Same Classifications	Equal Classifications	Exceptions
Lower Classifications	Seniority	Head Office
Work Group	Location	Site

Each of these contractual terms is invoked for the purposes of defining "bumping" rights and mobility entitlements of employees within each effected job category.

In 1991-92 the parties tried to move away from their traditional adversarial relationship into a more modern, interest-based and facilitated model of cooperative negotiations. As discussed below, they achieved some success, producing a Purchased Services Agreement along with initial steps at local labour management change initiatives in the nuclear units.

In 1993-94, Ontario Hydro began a major downsizing with a concomitant process of labour adjustment and dislocation. Total reduction in the work force has been approximately 12,000 employees — thirty-four per cent (34%) — over two years. Most of the reduction has come in the non-unionized staff, outside of the PWU and Society bargaining units, as the following chart shows:

Ontario Hydro Total Staff Levels
(1992-1994)

Employee Group	Sept. 1992	Feb. 1995	Reduction Staff	%
Executive	708	457	251	35
Non-represented	2275	1297	978	43
Society	7601	5388	2213	29
PWU	18,220	14,332	3888	221
Other	126	45	81	64
Total- Regular	28,930	21,519	7411	26
Non-Regular	1331	214	1117	84
Construction	4342	1110	3232	74
Total	34,603	22,843	11,760	34

(Ontario Hydro, 1994)

Under enormous financial and reorganizational pressures, the parties resorted to traditional confrontation in 1993-94 as management aggressively sought a separate collective agreement for nuclear. The dispute was concluded with a temporary employment security agreement. As a result, Hydro and its bargaining agents have relied on traditional collective agreement mechanisms and very expensive buy-out programmes to achieve the targeted work force reductions.

The parties are now exploring new forms of cooperation. Traditional techniques may have worked in the past but due to their costs, financial and socio-economic impacts on workers face diminishing returns and limited supportability in the future. The parties must look for new ways to reduce both the social costs of job loss for individual workers as well as the overall expense of the work force reduction programmes used to date. Improved worker outcomes and reduced costs involve new approaches to labour adjustment and training, for both the internal labour market of the corporation and the external labour market of the broader economy.

Management Initiatives: Retirement and Buyout Offers

Hydro management sought to achieve its targets for downsizing through a large and generous set of severance, early retirement and separation programmes, offered in three phases.

Phase I involved an Early Retirement Allowance and Voluntary Separation Allowance offer. 1,582 employees elected to take these options. Just under five thousand employees took advantage of the Special Retirement Program and a Voluntary Separation Program offered in Phase II. A Special Separation Program offered in Phase III, sought an additional 2,200 reduction, but only about 1,000 staff took up the option. The following chart summarizes the outcomes:

Summary of Voluntary Reduction Programs

	Early Retirement Allowance (ERA)	Voluntary Separation Allowance (VSA)	Special Retirement Program (SRP)	Voluntary Separation Program (VSP)
Employees	1399	183	2387	2598
Total Costs	149 M	6 M	33 M	110 M
Cost/ Employee	$106,500	$32,800	$181,400	$42,300

The numbers in the chart indicate significant, if diminishing successes, but achieved at very high costs. Few other employers possess the capacity to pass on the costs and afford such generous arrangements.

Union Initiatives: Protecting Job Security

The Power Worker's Union sought to deal with the risks and costs of job losses through three key traditional collective bargaining agreement mechanisms: Article 11 of the collective agreement on Surplus Staff Procedure, Article 13 on the Employment Security Plan and the 1994 Purchased Services Agreement. The type of procedure involved is reflected in Article 11.2 of the agreement:

> Depending on the business need of the location, where a surplus is identified in a classification at any location, either

the least senior regular part-time or the least senior regular full-time employee in the surplus classification in the location shall be declared surplus. Where the least senior employee is required to perform work which cannot be performed by a more senior employee in the location within four weeks, then the next senior employee within that classification shall be declared surplus.

Where there is more than one employee in a surplus classification at the same location, employees in the surplus classification at the location who are not surplus by virtue of their seniority may be given surplus status for vacancy purposes only. When the surplus has been eliminated or when the search/notice period has elapsed such surplus status shall be withdrawn.

Following each step in this procedure takes a long time and often involves "cross-bumping" of junior employees. In the face of the pervasive downsizing and uncertainty about future internal jobs, an extensive pool of employees under notice of surplus has accumulated. In the Customer Services business unit, the pool of surplus employees currently totals some 500 individuals.

In addition, an Employment Security clause was agreed to in 1994, which reads:

For the period April 1, 1994 to March 31, 1996, no regular Power Worker's Union-represented employees will be involuntarily terminated (does not include termination for cause or retirement at normal retirement age). During this time period, staff who are currently surplus or become surplus shall have their search/notice period extended to the earlier of placement in a vacancy/placement opportunity or March 31, 1996. Staff declared surplus on or after December 11, 1995 shall receive a minimum 16-week or 4-week search notice as described in Article 11.4.

To relieve the pressure on payroll costs created by the employment security provision, the parties agreed to reduce the Employer's pension fund contribution by a total of $200 million. (Ontario Hydro 1994) As a tactical move, reliance on a temporary employment security agreement and use of pension monies is understandable, but it is not a long-range solution. By definition, the parties can only go to the pension surplus a limited number of times. Nor do the intricate and cumbersome mechanisms of prolonged bumping rights and entitlements under Article 11 provide a long-range solution. At best they buy some time for adjustment and change.

Management's Historical Perspective

In management's view, the system evolved from 1985-87, a time of significant restructuring without downsizing. Workers were transferred within the organization, utilizing the contractual work rules which functioned reasonably well in internal re-deployment across complex job classifications and work units.

Management representatives acknowledge that the collective agreement is not able to deal with major downsizing. The sheer scale and nature of the changes means that the process is bogged down in procedural steps. Article 11 worked, in management's view, until the major downsizing and reorganization of the corporation. These require fundamental changes in approach to the collective agreement, addressed in part by the management proposal for a separate agreement for the nuclear unit. However, there was no consensus to change Article 11 in the 1994-96 collective agreement. A new contract provision on Employment Security was agreed to for the life of the agreement, taking some pressure off Article 11 through a moratorium on major dislocations. The key provision is the one quoted above.

The heart of the problem is the basic approach to jobs, skills and work organization. Individual management representatives agree that the Wagner industrial union model has applied at Hydro, even more so for management than for the union. Both the Society and the PWU have sought greater employee involvement, but many in management have resisted. On the other hand, management perceives that the union's model of a consensus corporation is one in which the PWU would hold a veto over all key decisions.

For Hydro management, in 1992-94 the PWU made a major gain through the Purchased Services Agreement which established a joint union-management process with respect to contracting out. Management believes the Purchased Services Agreement has been used by PWU as a broad veto device, to give leverage to their position on issues not related to contracting out.

With regard to future human resource management (HRM) strategies, management representatives realize that decisions involving fundamental choices over business strategies will have to be made, but the directions of those decisions have not yet been set. Upstream, substantial competition is expected. The corporation may shift its resources and emphasis Downstream and to the Grid. Most employees are Upstream and vulnerable to dislocation. The shift would also involve the professionalization of all employee groups and movement away from the traditional labour contract work organization and seniority rules.

Union's Historical Perspective

The PWU view of the recent history is not dissimilar from management in its description of the overall directions and current practices of the parties, but the union perceives the problem as inconsistency. In the 1980s, the management mentality was that Ontario Hydro was bigger than the government and money was not an issue. The labour-management relationship was traditional. At the end of the 1980s, this changed, primarily caused by the regulatory side, in the union's view, because of concerns raised by the Atomic Energy Control Board (AECB) about the nuclear operations including industrial relations hostility, morale, safety and efficiency. In correspondence, AECB expressed that had certain Hydro nuclear facilities been operating in the U.S., they would have been shut down by the regulatory authorities because of risks associated with accidents, backlog of maintenance work required and near misses. There was an implicit threat of lifting Hydro's nuclear operating licenses unless new behaviour was forthcoming.

In reaction, the union states that management looked to total quality management as a one-off solution and introduced an ambitious programme of quality improvement in the nuclear sector in

1990. For the Power Workers' Union, this represented an opportunity to engage in the change process as equal partners. There would be joint committees operating by consensus, meaning the union could have a veto. This "veto," in fact, has become the union's standard for assessing involvement across the corporation. Started in the 1990-92 period of cooperation, by 1993-94 the union had begun to get local buy-in by employees and engagement in the workplace.

In the period of cooperation, the parties also dealt with contracting out, the major issue in a 1985 work stoppage which went to arbitration. The arbitrator imposed a twenty-five per cent (25%) rule limiting the extent of contracting out without union agreement, but without an enforcement provision. Between 1985 and 1992 the union found it virtually impossible to monitor and police the provision. As a result, a mid-term working group was established to deal with contracting out. They had a facilitator involved and eventually agreed to the previously-mentioned Purchased Services Agreement. This was just prior to the 1992 official bargaining round.

During the 1992 negotiations, the parties dealt, among other things, with differences and differentiation across what are now the separate business units. There are different sections of the collective bargaining agreement to deal with working conditions in the various business units and they have been there a long time. They are usually dealt with by sub-committees, but because there is little incentive to settle, the pattern was erratic. In 1992, they used facilitators and problem-solving techniques and all sub-committees settled for the first time.

According to the PWU, in the 1994 negotiations management flipped back into adversarialism and decided to try to bust the union. The corporation announced pre-conditions for negotiations in the form of a $200 million concessions target and a separate collective agreement for the nuclear business unit. The PWU and the company both know the bargaining leverage of the nuclear operators who support all the other employee groups' demands. Consequently, the union called a council meeting, changed their constitution and put in place a strike mandate, receiving a ninety-eight per cent (98%) strike mandate. As a partial concession, the union allowed management to place a separate collective agreement for nuclear on the agenda as a demand, but not as a pre-condition for the talks.

Job protection was the PWU priority in 1994. They were willing to pay the price to keep the jobs, particularly because in this estimate, the wage bill was only six per cent (6%) of the total operating cost for Hydro. The key tradeoff was the employment security commitment for PWU members for the duration of the collective agreement. The mathematics and economics were straight forward: about 500 PWU members were vulnerable. They multiplied this amount of salary for two years and arrived at $200 million which they took out of the pension fund surplus. The limitations of this solution have been discussed.

PWU on Decentralization: A Participatory Proposal

The PWU has sought to deal with decentralization of the corporation through its own structure. There are consultative boards for each business unit and, at each plant, there are joint steering committees of each side. At the most senior level, decision-makers on each side are well aware of the issues concerning their relationship and employee involvement. There is a traditional Joint Committee on the Relationship and a new Employee Representative Involvement. The sides are close to agreement on the principles and procedures for activities in these forums.

The PWU has developed a comprehensive Involvement Policy on how they will approach discussions of employee involvement and restructuring.

It is the PWU's belief that Ontario Hydro should be a leader in the province of Ontario in workplace reforms directed at full employee involvement. To achieve this, a redesigning of the workplace is necessary so that it becomes less authoritarian, more democratic and safer. Recognizing this, the PWU will enter into negotiations with Ontario Hydro to develop a plan that will lead to full employee involvement in the business. (PWU 1994) In the union's view, this will require:
- substantial changes in how work is organized
- a significant reduction in bureaucracy and other associated overheads

- creation of opportunities for employees to identify and solve operating problems
- continued upgrading of skills of PWU represented members
- opportunity for full and meaningful involvement in all decisions. (PWU 1994)

For the Power Workers Union, a plan to achieve a workplace that continually improves fairness, performance and safety of operation will need to include:

- provisions for workers to have greater influence, accountability with necessary responsibility and control over the day to day operations of their workplace with all decisions at the operating unit level made by consensus
- development of managers who emphasize coaching and coordinating
- a workforce trained in safe work practices
- continual improvements in efficiency based on working more effectively, using improved equipment and technology and less waste.
- flattening the organization, elimination of unnecessary layers of management, administration and overhead costs. (PWU, 1994)

The union also proposes stringent rules for participation. In its view, the new workplace structure will require the full participation of PWU members to take advantage of their first-hand knowledge and experience. Full participation of the members, will require a plan which:

- premises participation on their knowledge and any resulting performance improvements will not result in direct or indirect loss of employment
- jointly develops and administers the process for redesigning the workplace and implementation of participation programs
- jointly develops structure and content of training programs and materials used in any course
- cannot be used to bypass the normal union structure, interfere or usurp authority of the grievance procedure, or interfere with any collective agreement or process
- cannot be used to discipline employees

- has only voluntary participation at all times. (PWU 1994)

PWU has proposed an ambitious and aggressive approach to participatory change. No doubt there will be adaptation as the parties discuss an actual protocol for involvement. A cynical view might be that the union, in the context of the conditions it seeks to impose on the process, is seeking a no-risk approach to change. On the other hand, the difficult recent history is alive in people's memories. Equally daunting is the search for clarity on what the other side of a new deal might be.

The Costs of Unemployment: Rational Insistence on Job Security

The strength of resistance to work force reductions by PWU-represented employees and their bargaining agents, and consequently their defense of conventional job classification and work rules, is economically rational when measured by a very concrete outcome measure that employees intuitively understand: the social and economic costs of job loss. What does the average PWU member risk if he or she loses their job?

Because neither the union nor Hydro management currently track employees after they leave the corporation, only estimates are possible. Using data from other sources, a "back of the envelope" answer to the question is:

Estimated Costs of Job Loss
for PWU Members
(Current $ per Year)

Male Worker	$9084
Female Worker	$11,367

(based on grade 12 education, 18 years at Hydro, semi-skilled)

It must be stressed that these are the income losses if workers find another job. In addition, the risks of unemployment for a typical PWU member is twenty-seven to forty-one per cent (27-41%) for males and twenty-seven to forty-six per cent (27-46%) for females, estimates based on the Ontario Ministry of Labour Adjustment Model. (Ontario Ministry of Labour 1993) The Ministry conducted a research project to track 1200 randomly selected workers through three years of post-layoff experience. They concluded that the burden of difficult labour market adjustments is concentrated on those who had a major investment in the jobs they lost, both in terms of long tenure and very specific skills not easily marketed to potential employers in today's labour market. (For more detail see Appendix 2.) The problem is exacerbated when the displaced worker has a limited amount of education. Also, women, all other factors being the same, can expect to face more difficult adjustment than men. (Ontario Ministry of Labour 1993) In all these respects, the PWU-represented employees are uniquely vulnerable to excessive economic losses if they lose their Hydro jobs.

Ministry of Labour Model
Economics Losses Due to Job Loss

Each year of tenure at displacement reduces earnings two to three years later by $132 per year in real terms. Put differently, those with long tenure — fifteen or more years with the same employer — will earn at least $2,000 a year less. Displaced workers in the broad occupational group "semi-skilled factory production operatives" earned $2,977 less in their last job than the reference group. Compared with the reference group of college and university graduates, those who have less than a Grade 8 education earn $8,693 less, those with full primary school $4,723 less, some high school $4,283 less, high school graduates $3,731 less and those with some college or university $2,643 less. And, after controlling for all the other factors that explain the post-displacement earnings differential — the fact of being a woman costs the displaced worker an additional $2,283. (Ontario Ministry of Labour 1993)

The Ministry of Labour model suggests the sorts of outcomes that dislocated PWU members may face. Given the importance of such economic risks to collective bargaining over Hydro restructuring in the coming years, it is in the parties' interests to do a tracking study on actual outcomes. Documenting the outcomes should be a first step to changing them.

Restructuring Potential: Revamping Human Resource Management

The Wagner industrial union model is part of the ambient operating environment in both the public and private sectors of the Canadian economy. At Ontario Hydro, it has served both parties' interests in the past, but the future requires evolving the collective bargaining and workplace relationship in more cooperative, participatory and productive directions. Most everyone will now agree that consultation is good, and involving employees and improving working conditions and skills are productive. However, at the end of the day, it is necessary to quantify the impacts of human resource management techniques, both to inform everyone on when and where progress is being made and to send better signals to the bargaining table on potential tradeoffs.

Some of the most advanced and creative econometric work on productivity impacts of human resource policies has been done on the steel industry, which, along with the auto assembly plant, is a reigning metaphor of the classical industrial age. One study quantifies the effects of human resource management practices on productivity and quality. (Ichniowksi 1993) The authors examine the impact of a series of human resource management variables including:

- incentive pay
- recruiting and selection
- teamwork and cooperation
- employment security
- flexible job assignment
- knowledge and skill training
- communications
- labour relations

The study revealed that taken separately, these individual actions have only minor impacts on productivity. When "clusters" of practices reinforce one another it has much greater impact. Four main clusters or systems of human resource management practices correspond to clear choices for what kind of labour-management regime Hydro, or any other employer, wishes to pursue. The first is the Traditional, or adversarial model discussed previously. In the second, Communications model, the attempt is made to involve the union in consultation and increase the information flow to employee groups, but not to change the basic structure of the workplace or the labour agreement. Employee work groups are re-organized around teams, given new training and opportunities to coordinate activities differently than the traditional top-down management approach in the Teamwork model. Finally, in a High Performance model, the whole approach to employee involvement is combined with changes to the basic compensation system and overall human resource management system.

If the four systems are designated Traditional-HRM1; Communications-HRM2; Teamwork-HRM3; High Performance-HRM4; the measurable impact on productivity of each of these HRM models is summarized in the following table:

HRM Model	Productivity Outcome	Quality Outcome
HRM1	Trend Line	Trend Line
HRM2	2%	4%
HRM3	3.5%	4%
HRM4	7.5%	13%

It is not possible to make immediate generalizations to the entire private industrial sector, let alone to the public sector, from one specialized study of the steel industry. However, the study certainly suggests directions for future research on the potential for productivity gains from innovative workplace practices. It also suggests directions for progressive movement from the Wagner industrial model to a more participatory and higher performance model.

Steel mills and power plants share attributes of high fixed costs, high capital intensity and traditionally organized work forces. An initial estimate is that each one per cent (1%) productivity improvement in a nuclear station brings the corporation an additional $25 million in revenue. Ontario Hydro parties have major opportunities for mutual gains through development of new joint human resource initiatives. If these results are even generally applicable, they point to hundreds of millions of dollars in savings available to the parties if they could agree to pursue alternative human resource practices and re-align their industrial relations practices to match. That is the good news. The bad news is that one-off solutions produce meagre results unless they are associated with general changes or clusters of new policies. This means that in isolation, quality improvement initiatives by management or employment security proposals by the union, are unlikely to be sustainable successes.

This research indicates a direction and potential. Further analysis, with application to Hydro facilities, is needed to document the potential for gains and quantify the trade-offs for the parties.

Restructuring Lessons: Electricity Commission of New South Wales

The transformation underway at Ontario Hydro is not unique. The process of change in the regulatory, technology and operating environment is underway in the electric utility industry world-wide. A helpful example may be taken from the New South Wales (NSW), Australia, Electricity Commission.

A five-year-long process of redesign and dialogue with bargaining agents has resulted in major progress on workplace reform. The move into autonomous business units has been generally similar to Ontario Hydro. For management, this has been linked to a focus on results and performance agreements, through which local management will be accountable. On the employee side, there has been a change in work organization linked to retraining and entry into work teams and workplace consultative committees.

The whole NSW Electricity Commission has been consolidated into a single salary structure consisting of forty job grades, within which there are six salary bands. (Electricity Commission 1990) Each power worker has a Skills Development and Career Path. Over 130 non-trade classifications are being consolidated into four new multi-skilled non-trades groups.

New Structure and Career Path

Probationary Work	Level 4	PW4
Power Worker	Level 3	PW3
Power Worker 2	Level 2	PW2
Power Worker 1	Level 1	PW1
Power Line Worker	Level A	PLW

(NSW Electricity Commission 1990)

When the restructuring process is fully implemented, all existing non-trade employees will be reclassified as power workers. Training will be provided in accordance with a certified skill development plan. In broad terms, Ontario Hydro and the PWU could fruitfully pursue a similar track — major consolidation of job classifications in association with new, jointly-administered retraining programs for employees.

Sector Model of Adjustment

Part of the underlying issue in labour adjustment at Ontario Hydro is whether both parties — management and labour — take real ownership for the process and outcomes. The parties will not be able to deal successfully in new and cooperative ways with the internal restructuring of the workplace — including reskilling, work re-organization and career planning — until they jointly take ownership and co-manage the external labour market outcomes. In the absence of this joint effort, both sides are consigned to a war of attrition over current collective agreement mechanisms in which all parties, including the public, suffer sub-optimal outcomes, to say the least.

New sectoral partnerships dealing with labour adjustment and training have emerged in recent years across Canada as a focal point for labour and management doing their business differently and together in the future. (Haddad 1995) Sectoral councils have been established in most of Canada's major industries including steel, electrical and electronics, automotive parts, automotive repair and service, aviation maintenance, graphic arts, software development, and hospitals and health care. They continue to grow in popularity. According to one estimate, thirty-five sector groups existed in some stage of formation in 1992. Government's willingness to fund the councils reflects a belief that industry and labour leaders are best able to define the human resource needs of the workplaces they represent, and to design programs for effectively responding to these challenges. Moreover, it is recognized that these councils represent a strategic and coordinated method for developing comprehensive human resource strategies.

After years of academics preaching to practitioners about Japanese or European models on labour-management cooperation, in the late 1980s, Canadian labour and management started to generate a home-grown model of labour-management cooperation and change. This model allows labour and management to come together outside the confines of the traditional collective bargaining relationship, without seeking to end-run the normal bargaining process. The primary objective is to have the parties co-manage labour markets in new ways. Inevitably, the first and primary focus will be retraining and redeployment of employees displaced as industries and sectors restructure. This will not just involve external redeployment from an existing employer to a new employer, but will also involve internal redeployment to different operations or occupations within an existing employer. Labour and management will need to address the human resource policies and strategies of the current employer jointly. The necessary extension of the process will be for the labour and management to address long-range human resource strategies for their organizations and industries.

At the conclusion of this process private sector labour and management will exert as much energy negotiating the definition and implementation of the future skill set of their work force, as they have, in the past, on employee compensation. Though these ideas are new to the public sector, they are commonplace, yet leading edge developments in the private sector. What has been said of the new economy is that in an era of increased mobility of capital and technology the primary competitive advantage of nations is the skills of their people and the ability to innovate. (Reich 1991) If the public sector is to contribute what we require for our quality of life and our future economic competitiveness then these maxims must not only apply to private firms and industries, they must apply equally to public institutions.

The analogy for Hydro from the private sector council experience would be to establish a similar body to deal with active labour market policy across Hydro's diverse operations, and ultimately with the Ontario electric utility industry as a whole. The project offers three potential benefits:

- **Economies of Scale and Scope**

    Hydro's current efforts rely on the implicit assumption that the adjustment problem can be handled within its own operations. It currently seeks to offer counselling, transition assistance and training to employees under surplus notice. Hydro has offered passive measures such as early retirement and voluntary severance offers which as the data indicate, had early success but now faces very large cumulative costs and diminishing returns. PWU members, among others, do not feel that they have any alternate employment and career opportunities. A natural opportunity lies with other utilities, where ex-Hydro staff have often gone in the past. There may also be additional opportunities with Hydro customers. Extending the scope to a sectoral council including broader utilities can spread the costs further and access any government funds available to assist in deferring the costs.

- **Joint Management of Worker Transitions**

    As discussed above, currently neither Hydro management nor the union take any responsibility for workers after they have left the corporation. No one knows the true outcomes, beyond personal anecdotes, because there is no tracking data. More fundamentally however, external labour market outcomes and internal labour market regulation under collective agreements are intimately linked. PWU members hold strongly to their present positions out of fear of having no alternative. This creates additional pressures to increase internal labour market rigidities through more and more restrictive and expensive contract provisions like the Purchased Services and Employment Security agreements. Hydro's corporate objective of greater internal flexibility and mobility of employees and skills is unlikely to be achieved as long as the outcome for PWU members remains a twenty-five per cent (25%) loss of income and twenty-five to forty per cent (25-40%) unemployment rates.

- **Bridges to Joint Human Resource Practices**
  At times, individuals within Hydro management and the PWU talk about achieving a cooperative goal of a high-skill, high-wage workplace where employees have active participation in their business units and expansive career plans as "knowledge workers." The experience across Canada has been that, to achieve a new "flexibility-security" deal of this type, new structures of labour-management cooperation are required in which the management and union come together as equal partners in new ways. The sector council model is the best current example which can make this an achievable goal.

This chapter has discussed the current efforts of Ontario Hydro to successfully downsize in a way that meets its operational and financial objectives, while also dealing with employees as fairly and humanely as possible. A series of management retirement and voluntary severance arrangements have been introduce with significant aggregate accomplishments. The PWU, in turn, has sought to safeguard the job security interests of their membership with aggressive new contract guarantees. To deal with the on-going process of internal and external redeployment of Hydro staff however, will require additional and new approaches. The restrictive job classification and work rule provisions in the collective agreement are there precisely to prevent the huge potential income and social losses that have been estimated for dislocated Hydro workers. To find a new flexible and effective approach for its unionized employees will require moving on both the collective bargaining and active, joint labour adjustment fronts. Labour and management representatives at Hydro would be well-advised to look at an adaptation of the sector council model to establish a new partnership in positive cooperation and human resource planning.

The sheer scale and geographic scope of Hydro's operations means that they can and need to turn these to advantage. Hydro needs to widen the scope to move people into new career paths on an on-going basis outside the restrictive cycle of bargaining a new contract every three years in a ritual dance.

Ontario Hydro and Privatization

The Macdonald Report (1996) has recommended that Hydro operations should be further split and some parts should be privatized to encourage competition. However, the expectation is not that Hydro will simply convert from a government utility to a private for-profit firm. Whatever the future structure, it will take place along a spectrum of organizational choices and delivery agents. For Hydro and other government operations, "privatization" is not likely to be a simple matter of in or out. The spectrum is best thought of in terms of the following matrix:

	Budget Sector		Market Sector	
	Public	Private	Public	Private
Non-Profit	1	2	3	4
For Profit	5	6	7	8

As the matrix states, public services are provided by a mix of organizations, some relying on direct government budgets and transfers, and others on market prices. A government department would fall into cell #1, a privately incorporated, non-profit public hospital into #2. Ontario Hydro, as a crown corporation, has occupied cell #3, a publicly-owned, non-profit selling to markets. What now proposed is the splitting up of Hydro into a series of separate units occupying various cells across #4 through #8. The new Grid may occupy cell #4 if it is a co-venture with the municipal utilities. New co-generation operators will be a combination of non-profits and for-profit private firms covering cells #3, 4 and 7. Commercialized Hydro operations may be converted into cell #8. The fundamental point is that for Hydro and elsewhere in the public sector, there is currently a spectrum of service delivery agents and this will continue in the future. Most of what takes place under the label of "privatization" will occur as a shift from cell #2 through #7, rather than a radical leap from #1 to #8.

Finally, the Macdonald Report also recommends active employee and bargaining agent involvement in the process of change. Squaring the circle between this and the commitment to privatization will require qualitatively new collective bargaining and human resource policies at Hydro. There is no way to get there from here, in the existing relationships and contractual arrangements.

— CHAPTER 6 —
HARD CHANGES, NEW BARGAINS:
Transforming Public Sector Labour-Management Relations

In the 1980s, a widely acclaimed book, *The Transformation of American Industrial Relations* argued that American private sector labour-management relations were undergoing a fundamental shift. Changes in the international economy and in technology, combined with anti-union sentiment in the business community and a redistribution of managerial authority away from centralized corporate human resource structures was shifting both the location and terms of the labour-management interface. Strategic union responses required learning lessons from new approaches. A decade-long perspective, as discussed earlier, saw the traditional Wagnerist paradigm of private sector labour-management relations move toward greater emphasis on joint partnerships. The shop floor of most modern factories looks more like a computer or testing lab than like Henry Ford's original production line. The change process has not been easy nor has it arrived at a single, congenial resting place, but the direction and the progress are clear, if only in retrospect.

In the 1990s, the public sector labour-management system is undergoing a similar system transformation. The economic environment has altered fundamentally and permanently. Managerial authority is being shifted outward and downward, away from centralized bureaucracies and toward dispersed operating organizations. New approaches to service delivery are emerging. To date, the trade union response has focused primarily on political opposition and demonstrations against privatization and contracting out. This response is understandable and justifiable in terms of the imminent threats to union members' jobs and pervasive economic insecurity. However, at the end of the day *unions are what they negotiate*. The key will be what happens at public sector bargaining tables *and* what enlightened management has to offer in a deal.

What differentiates public sector labour-management relations from those in the private sector is the option of *political exit*. While government can simply leave a particular field or close a service, it is rarely the case that a private sector organization will voluntarily exit a market or product line. Political exit — defined in detail below — has become an active option for political decision-makers. The familiar call of "We're out of here" echoes when budgets hit an impasse.

The general movement towards more decentralization and commercialization can be described as lying on a continuum between a traditional government department and a private, for-profit firm operating in the marketplace. Movement from one end of the continuum to the other is privatization in its most extreme form and, in fact, amounts to political exit. When a function previously supplied by a government organization, say geological mapping, is no longer delivered by public organizations or public employees and so far as geological mapping continues, it is delivered by private firms for a market price without public subsidy, there is no transformation of public sector employment relations. The service is simply gone from the public sector.

Traditional Wagnerist devices for dealing with this sort of privatization threat are restrictions on contracting out in collective agreements and labour board remedies through successor rights which transfer employee wages, benefits, contract and union rights to the new employer. Where employees are unionized, they and their bargaining agents will pursue the remedies available under successor rights provisions of relevant labour law. These are the two traditional blunt instruments in union hands, but the target they are meant for may not appear.

It is not likely that this form of privatization will be the standard, let alone the dominant, case in Canada. More likely, there will be various movements to subsidiary operating units in government or transfer agencies and to some form of public or private, for-profit or non-profit, organization. Movement from traditional government units to other contracted agencies, but short of market-based private firms, represents the majority case and the true possibility for transformation of public sector labour-management relations.

Analysis of collective agreements, however, reveals that, over the last decade, the public sector has been moving in a direction which more deeply embeds the Wagner model of job control unionism, shoring up Henry Ford's mass production model regarding delivery of public services. As stated earlier, employee groups and bargaining agents that attempt to retain, let alone extend, the mass production model will be most in danger of chronic downward wage pressure and contracting out in the future.

Workers and their unions have a strategic interest in the transformation of the workplace and renewal of public services. The irony is that the threat of political exit leaves the union leader and management counterparts knowing exactly what they should do. It is the challenge of transforming labour-management relations — redrawing jobs and skills — which leaves people much more confused.

Trade Unions and Employee Involvement

Public sector Wagnerism is not the only problem in the Canadian public sector's troubled future. Active employees and employee organization involvement are critical to viable and effective public services. Trade unions, employers, government and employees will have to take individual and collective decisions about the kind of employment relations they want in their future.

The underlying issue is employee representation and voice in the public sector enterprise. It is also a question of what, not whether change comes. A democratic society, particularly one with twenty-four-hour mass media and information flows, will never have completely unregulated labour markets. The days of child labour, exploitation, industrial pollution and carnage, along with unilateral employment relations, ended with the close of the nineteenth century and are not returning. In a democracy there are three ways to regulate labour markets and employment relations: the traditional union model; a new professional employee association or employee involvement scheme; or the courts. One of these choices will be made, either actively or by default.

The decline of unionization in the private sector, particularly in the United States, has led to much speculation about the end of unions. Some postulate that public sector unions may follow on the same track. What does the future hold? Informed observers point to a "participation gap" in the modern workplace and workforce. A series of studies confirms that for all age, sex, race, occupation, education and earnings groups, a *representation* or *participation gap* exists between what employees believe they can contribute at the workplace and what current work organizations allow them to do. Two-thirds of respondents say that they "would like to have more influence" in workplace decisions. The majority favour joint co-operation committees with management. Given a choice of union "yes" or "no," a substantial number choose "yes." Given a more complex choice between two institutions — co-operative committees or unions — a proportion of those who favour unions shift towards the committee option and those who do not want unions also choose the committee option. (Freeman 1995)

The attitude of employers towards unions is negative. They favour new forms of management-initiated employee involvement (EI) committees which "empower" workers to make workplace decisions. EI takes many forms — teams, quality circles, total quality management — introduced because employers believe that employee involvement is profitable. But, can EI succeed in the absence of an independent employee organization to protect employee interests? Opinions and research studies vary, but the weight of evidence is that independent employee organizations contribute more to sustainable, productive and profitable organizations' success.

What is the government's interest in workplace representation? In the United States, the absence of trade unions has created a social vacuum that has generated pressures for laws regulating management behaviour, and produced a wave of court cases and complaints to government agencies about employment rights. The dramatic drop in the level of union membership over the last twenty years has been matched by a more than four hundred per cent (400%) increase in the number of law suits dealing with employment disputes. Fully sixteen per cent (16%) of all cases in U.S. district courts are now about employment issues. If employees can only gain protection through the state, they will press legislatures for that protection and use courts and agencies to enforce their rights. All of which leads to the conclusion that one way or another there will be a renewal of employee representation, though not necessarily one associated with traditional unions.

Implications for Public Sector Trade Unions and Labour-Management Relations

For public sector trade unions, the established mind set is that Wagnerism is the only way for unions to provide a strong and independent employee voice. To the extent that they maintain this position, public sector trade unionists will paint themselves and their members into a corner. Defending the traditional approach to job structures and work rules to the death will be a losing strategy in the long run. As mentioned earlier, where it is tried it will be beset by chronic pressures to contract out or privatize to save costs. The communications and bargaining strategy of the unions has been based on the now vulnerable premise that the welfare state is deeply imbedded in the population, and that the economic interests of their members are synonymous with the interest of the service clients and other citizens. This economic rationale underlies the trade union political coalition strategy. The deepening of populist fiscal conservatism is rapidly eroding the power of this position. The union side will have to come up with a new economic argument and a bargaining strategy. The fulcrum of that strategy will have to be a new deal on the re-organization of work and service delivery.

Public sector employers do not have an unassailable hand either. Employer unilateralism will not work. To deliver high quality services and reduce costs, employers need an active, committed work force. In terms of the industrial models, hospitals, school boards and municipalities will have to become high-performance workplaces with motivated work forces: the equivalent of the union co-managed enterprise at GM's Saturn in operations. From the other side, public sector management will have to live with the risk of political exit if they don't perform. If the service exits, management supervisors and non-union employees will also be out on the street. A new, high-performance model for public sector service delivery is not yet in sight, at least not in Canada. Until it comes into view, management negotiators will not be able to frame a new deal at the bargaining table and public sector unions will have no offer to bargain around, even when they are so disposed.

Governments also have a direct interest in the forms of employee participation and representation as they emerge, an interest that is larger than their narrow fiscal one. Without the emergence of a new labour-management and employee representation system, the future will yield more direct government regulation and greater resort to the courts. Were Canada to experience the rise in court-based employment relations that has emerged in the American private sector, it will be even more litigious than the private sector because Canadian public sector employment law overall is more highly regulated. Over the last ten years, regulations such as employment equity have been built into the culture of public sector workplaces and the expectations of employees. These expectations will not evaporate. Without a new model, more will resort to legislation, regulatory agencies and the courts, creating two major problems for government. By regulatory proxy they will again become the employer of all public sector workers and will wind up, in the early twenty-first century, directly managing all the public sector service delivery, after spending late 1990s trying to distance themselves from this role. It is well-established that court-based and regulatory-based employment relations are even more costly and inflexible than the traditional union model.

The punch lines are quite clear. Reform of public sector services is better than wholesale contracting out and complete privatizing. And, more effective and involved employee representation produces superior results to alienation and the courts.

Bargaining Strategically in the Public Sector

Public sector collective bargaining is entering a new era in an economic environment that is dramatically different from the one in which it was framed, and in a context of vulnerable public services. While many parties may simply try to extend existing collective agreements with informal understandings to apply them differently — fewer staff with the same job classifications, pruning benefits and premiums — others will "add-on" to the existing labour-management machinery. Instead a whole new approach is needed.

Australia, which has been undergoing similar change over the past decade, offers a glimpse of the future, with a "Westminster" political system, a large public sector and high union density. Canada will experience the same shift in the industrial relations system, away from centralism and towards local service-related bargaining as has already come to the "enterprise agreement" system in Australia. This is more than a locational shift. It is a fundamental change in the perception and culture of public sector labour-management relations toward local agreements — a change that can drive continuous improvement in service delivery.

Current calls for more flexibility in collective agreements are not just part of a neo-conservative political cycle which will pass away in another turn of the political cycle. Neither will they be protested or politically lobbied away. For unions to avoid marginalization, the public sector bargaining programme will have to alter qualitatively. The following table compares the major categories in current collective agreements with the collective agreement of the future.

Collective Agreement of the Future

What's There Now	What's Needed	Description
Management's Rights	Quality	Quality standards, timeliness, cost
Grievance Procedures	Competence	Competency standards, multi-skilling, future needs
Job Classifications	Financial	Program costs, staff costs, delivery costs
Work Rules	Service Delivery	Work processes, team work, customer service
Wage Rates	Equity	Access to promotion, staff distribution, competency attainment

(Adapted from Graham 1996)

At the heart of the change will be on-going re-examination and renewal of the format of work. Written job descriptions and work rules must serve less as a means to formalize rigidities and more as a means to measure and improve work processes. In continuous improvement, job descriptions and classifications, along with work rules, change to meet client demand. To return to where this book began, the central element in change is the new challenge to public sector Wagnerism and job control unionism. Unions must fundamentally shift their role. Without change, they face a downward spiral of marginalization and declining influence.

Public sector unions cannot be expected to negotiate without information or only talk to themselves on this new agenda. An equally daunting challenge faces the management side. Again, drawing from Australian experience, the following is a practical checklist of information that an open and competent management bargaining team needs to bring to the table *and to openly share with the union from the outset.*

Management Checklist for New Bargaining Agenda

Market Values

- Customer expectation & value for services & products
- Standards for services & products
- Cost of services & products

Work Culture

- Degree of co-operation between management & staff
- Degree of co-operation between categories of staff
- Degree of organizational standards versus external standards
- Obligations of management

Work Design

- Existing & required services & products
- Number of people involved in service & product delivery
- Work process to deliver each service & product
- Individual & unit's role in adding value to the service & product delivery
- Flexibility of individuals & units to adopt changed processes to meet new markets
- Equity & access
- Dispute prevention & resolution

Management Checklist for New Bargaining Agenda (cont'd)

- Obligations of staff
- Flexibility of the organization to initiate & respond to market demands
- Needs of individuals & needs of organization
- Equity & access
- Union representation

Workforce Requirements

- Staff numbers required to deliver services & products
- Competencies required to deliver services & products
- Sum of competencies currently held
- Allocation of competencies to work processes
- Multi-skilling & training
- Flexibility of individuals & units to acquire & apply a range of competencies to meet new markets
- Full-time, part-time, casual & contract staff
- Levels & categories of employment
- Equity & access

Hours of Operation

- Market demand
- Capacity
- Core hours, shift hours, overtime
- Equity & access
- Time off in lieu

Cost and Remuneration

- Rates of pay for all types of employment
- Types of leave
- Rest breaks
- Equity & access
- Contingency service
- Workers compensation
- Pensions
- Retrenchment & layoffs
- Work load
- Bonuses

Evaluation

- Productivity performance assessment of individuals & groups
- Process evaluation
- Market re-appraisal

(Adapted from Graham 1994)

Compared to the current minimal sharing of cursory financial information and strategic plans between management and unions in Canada, the checklist shows that a dramatic change in attitude, culture and psychology is needed on the management side.

The degree of change in the culture of labour-management relations, combined with the long change cycles of collective bargaining itself, mean we should not expect a new wave of collective agreements overnight. For the next five years, the parties will have their hands full managing and adapting to these changes. The real danger is in the lag effect. Cycles of collective bargaining are now seriously out of synch with cycles of fiscal change. This raises the issue of the underlying capacities for innovation in the public sector, of which labour-management is only one part, albeit a critical component.

Public Sector Innovation

In recent years, public sector management innovation has come to mean strategic planning, re-engineering, total quality management, benchmarking, team building and privatization. For labour-management relations, the most de-stabilizing of these innovations will be knee-jerk resorts or over-reliance on privatization. As pointed out earlier, ironically, if management simply resorts to privatization and contracting out, the union knows exactly what to do. Innovation, like the Australian example below, is much more challenging.

Transforming Labour-Management Relations in the Public Sector: State Government in New South Wales, Australia

In 1988, elections returned a government dedicated to running government "like an efficient and effective business" in the Australian state of New South Wales. Between 1988 and 1994 significant improvements were achieved including a smaller, more efficient government. State government employment declined from twelve to ten per cent (12 to 10%) of the total state labour force and turned the focus on customer needs, and better value services for tax dollars.

In the new system, market-testing and contracting-out reviews are mandatory elements of the formal budget planning process. Key objectives are:

- ensuring best value for money through competition
- creating savings which can be re-allocated to key priorities

- focusing more clearly on community needs
- greater flexibility through the use of contractors.

In contracting out, overall standards are maintained by requiring the contractor to follow government rules concerning equity, quality, probity, and accountability in public service delivery.

New South Wales is moving towards a "performance related culture" within the public sector which involves a new concentration on customer needs, feedback from the public, and developing clear goals and performance measures. General initiatives include the introduction of corporate and business planning, program statements, and TQM principles. The budget process is being similarly reworked to encourage more accurate financial reporting, an emphasis on the outcomes of government activities, and clearly defined roles and objectives for agencies.

The Australian state has also introduced a number of measures to encourage devolution of authority. Central agencies are increasingly responsible for policy development and regulation, while line agencies concentrate on service delivery. All agencies have experienced delayering and a further devolution of authority to lower levels of management. This has increased flexibility and has pushed decision-making closer to the point of contact with customers. Likewise, staffing priorities have been shifted from administration to direct service delivery.

What has all this meant for industrial relations? The *Public Sector Management Act, 1988* abolished the Public Service Board, transferring "people management" functions from this central authority to department heads. The Act also established the Senior Executive Service and reinforced the merit principle within the public service.

The Senior Executive Service introduced performance-based, fixed-term contracts paying market wages for senior managers and enhanced management development programs and opportunities for lateral recruitment and mobility.

The move away from central management of industrial relations increased the ability of agencies to tailor their human resource policies to their business objectives and improved customer service. Flexible hours and working conditions and broader classification systems have been introduced, with the underlying philosophy that:

> [t]he Government sees it as important for the well-being of our community to set an example, as an employer, of providing a greater choice for employees of practical, family friendly employment arrangements aimed at improved organizational effectiveness.

Moving from a "cost neutral" requirement for employer-sponsored child care to a "cost-effective" approach is an example of these arrangements. To support agencies in meeting their new labour-management responsibilities, the Australian government has established the Industrial Relations Consultancy as a central resource.

In 1992 "enterprise bargaining" was introduced. Enterprise bargaining devolves collective bargaining to local workplaces, encouraging local approaches to enhance productivity, improve service-delivery and stimulates performance rewards. It wants to create a better fit between agency goals and the individual "business priorities" and other needs of employees. Enterprise agreements must include grievance and dispute resolution processes and are limited in scope by overall legislated guidelines on sick leave, hours of work, and wage rates.

By 1994, 185,000 out of 300,000 public sector employees in the state were engaged in enterprise-level bargaining. While a small number of local agreements — covering only 1,000 staff — were registered under federal legislation, the rest are covered by fifty-one enterprise agreements under the New South Wales *Industrial Relations Act, 1991*.

The Perils of Privatization

Longitudinal studies of American experiences over the past decade show that privatization *only* makes sense after the organization has gone through a strategic planning process. Core functions, essential to the organization's reason for being, are the activities it can and should do itself. Necessary functions that are not central to the organization's definition of self may be privatized. For example, the U.S. Environmental Protection Agency's (EPA) Superfund toxic waste cleanup program contracts with private organizations for the clean-up of waste sites. No EPA staff actually performs clean-up work. But, decisions about where clean-up workers are assigned and how clean a site needs to be are made by EPA staffers. The allocation of work tells us what is central to EPA's mission — maintaining standards and accountability — and what is not.

Commentators stress other pitfalls of privatization. There is clear evidence that governments are better than private sector agencies at policy management, regulation, protecting sovereign interests, and ensuring continuity and stability of services. Governments have also historically led the private sector in preventing discrimination and exploitation, and in non-discriminatory hiring. The public sector employs a higher proportion of racial-ethnic workers and women than the private sector.

For any organization, a clearly-defined focus is essential. Once the focus is determined, the organization will increasingly strive to shed functions that are not central. Higher quality, more cost-effective work demands that an organization focus its resources on those functions central to its existence and shed or contract out secondary functions. Too often, privatization is not based on a clear strategic plan, but on expedience, to raise immediate cash for budget balancing, escape criticism for poor performance, or fit into the credo that the market cures all ills.

New Economic Assumptions

Unlike the private sector — where the pressures of international competition drive management toward union-busting or new human resource strategies to stay in business — in the public sector, politicians increasingly entertain exit from direct service provision as called for by much of the anti-government animus in the mass media. This pressure raises the fundamental issue of transforming public sector labour-management relations and seeking a new set of economic assumptions to underpin public sector collective bargaining. Traditional public sector Wagnerism has proceeded on Keynesian welfare state and demand management assumptions that are increasingly challenged from all sides.

Lurking behind much of the discussion of public sector industrial relations developments in Ontario and elsewhere is a furtive question of whether the fiscal crises will lead inevitably to the same precipitous decline in unionization seen in the North American private sector over the past 20 years. There are two conflicting views of the future. As stated above, one optimistic prognosis suggests reasons for qualified long range hope related to the participation/representation gap. (Freeman 1995)

In this scenario a new spurt in employee organization will result from unfulfilled demand for participation and representation in the workplace. If employees want greater representation/participation at their firms, as surveys indicate; if companies want greater employee involvement; and, if governments realize the advantages of regulating workplaces through local worker organizations, then the conditions would seem to be in place for a surge in worker representation and participation. The broader society, moreover, needs employee organizations to deal with the huge rise in earnings inequality and immiseration of low-skill workers characteristic of US and UK economic growth in the 1980s and 1990s. (Freeman 1995)

Other commentators argue that while the world is converging on the basis of market relations, and not, as previously expected, on the basis of organizational forms — we won't all work Toyota-style — this does not mean that the Anglo-American path of de-unionization is the path everyone else will follow. Instead, other organizational and political factors will generate different solutions. In the other view, it should not be assumed that workers, companies and government pursue a single objective, exclusive of all else. If workers ask for voice and high wage; if companies want employee involvement and anti-union policies; and if government is anti-union and pro-market, it is not evident that Freeman's compromise will be the solution. There is a much greater possibility of deadlock into an inefficient sub-optimal economic result. (Boyer 1995)

The first optimistic remark suggests a new, positive employee voice in organization, and an equity impulse in the economy. The second suggests a political deadlock under neo-conservatism. The recent political "successes" of Conservative governments in Alberta and Ontario suggest we are headed toward economic deadlock. All of this raises the question of a foundation for a different economics of public sector collective bargaining in the coming years.

Toward a New Economics of Collective Bargaining

Because it is impossible to separate organizational developments from economic context, a re-examination of the economic assumptions behind public sector Wagnerism is required. For most of the postwar period, public sector unionism and collective bargaining has been riding the back of the Keynesian assumption that the egalitarian policies of the welfare state, through the impact of redistribution on effective economic demand, created a virtuous circle of productivity growth in the economy. However, even leftist economists now acknowledge that the egalitarian policy prescriptions of traditional Keynesian theory do not survive close scrutiny. Both left-leaning and right-leaning economists now agree that sustained growth in income and employment depends on productivity.

The belief that wage increases along with expanding public social services and transfers stimulate aggregate demand and promote economic growth was central to Keynesianism. This belief was sustained by the rapid postwar growth in living standards in many countries pursuing egalitarian economic policies. Keynesianism holds that output is limited by aggregate demand. Egalitarian policies increase aggregate demand by redistributing income to those with a higher marginal propensity to spend. Egalitarian policy addresses the needs of the less well-off, stimulates economic growth and promotes abundance for all.

However, now econometric studies suggest that Keynesian "wage-led" growth is relatively ineffective and possibly counter-productive in open economies. Studies show that when Keynesian policies lead to an expansion of aggregate demand, they do not lead to increases in either the level of investment or the rate of productivity growth. Keynesian demand management is, at best, a short-term stabilization policy; necessary as a component of economic policy, but tangential to sustainable, long-term productivity growth. (Bowles & Gintis 1995)

In addition, in Ontario especially, the public sector union political strategy continues to proceed on the risky assumption that the welfare state is still firmly embedded in the political culture. This appears to be the reason the impressive round of labour-led demonstrations in 1995-96 against the Conservative government of Premier Mike Harris is expected to re-leverage union bargaining. Ironically, this strategy flies in the face of the difficult fact that union members voted for the Conservatives and their slash-the-deficit economic argument in the thousands.

Contrary to prevailing neo-conservative tenets, good economic arguments indicate that more egalitarian economic policies are a significant boost to long-run productivity growth. There are also strong arguments in favour of greater employee involvement, shared ownership of management and human resource development within the firm. (Bowles & Gintis 1995) However, to engage in this line of economic argument means a substantial move away from the traditions of job control unionism that continues to be the gold standard for most public sector unionists. But, unions cannot make deals alone, the other prospective partners — employers and government — have to want to play a new game.

Strategies for a New Era

In Ontario, the recent extraordinary shift in the governing party from the most left-wing government in the province's history to a radical neo-conservative administration illustrates the volatility of this dramatic period of public sector change. In a short period of time — less than three years — provincial labour-management relations have experienced the first public-services wide strike, the beginning of massive layoffs, an unsuccessful attempt at participatory change and resort to legislation overriding collective agreements.

Collective bargaining is characterized by more incremental decentralized change. To start re-aligning labour-management institutions, Ontario could benefit from the following new approaches:

- **Multi-partite Consultations**

    For each major component of the public sector, multi-partite consultations to define appropriate performance measurements should occur between governments, employers, unions and client groups.

- **Performance Improvement**

    A portion of provincial transfer grants for hospitals, municipalities and school boards should be linked to performance improvement. Agencies and local governments performing significantly above or below the performance norm — set at three per cent (3%) per year for the whole public sector — for their peers would be rewarded or penalized in subsequent years.

- **Two-tier Wage Increases**

    Where there is central wage-setting, central wage settlements and arbitration awards should be in two-tier increases, one half awarded across the board and the second half in relation to local productivity agreements. Guidelines for local productivity should be centrally defined.

- **Consolidation of Job Classifications**

    Consolidation of job classifications and simplification of work rules can be a major source of productivity improvement. Labour and management should re-examine their approaches to job classifications and simplification of work rules. Changes should be accompanied by employment security measures that improve employee placement in new jobs or locations.

- **Public Sector Workplace Survey**

    A public sector workplace survey across the government and broader public sector should be taken regularly to identify and monitor best practises in human resource policies and innovation. Results should be publicized through joint labour-management forums.

- **Sector Councils**
  Cooperative labour-management mechanisms to deal with labour adjustment, re-deployment and re-skilling for new service delivery approaches will be needed to deal with public sector restructuring. Public sector employers and unions should examine sector council experience in the private sector. Where labour and management agree to proceed with sector councils, government should facilitate and financially contribute to their efforts.

- **Restructuring Framework Agreements**
  Labour and management should negotiate restructuring framework agreements across existing bargaining units and collective agreements where hospitals, municipalities or educational institutions with multiple bargaining units are undergoing major restructuring. These agreements would provide employee mobility and re-deployment across existing bargaining unit and job classifications for dislocated employees.

- **Examine Separate Wage Arbitration Streams**
  Where separate wage arbitration schemes exist for different occupational groups within the same employer — for example, police, fire and nursing units within the same municipality — these should be re-examined. Large wage iniquities have emerged between these groups, often correlating with gender differences.

- **Multi-Employer Associations**
  Legislation or regulations should facilitate multi-employer associations within the broader public sector which can participate in sector councils, collective bargaining where appropriate and consultation on human resource development. Governments should disengage as the surrogate final employer across the broader public sector.

- **Training in New Collective Bargaining**
  Government should provide limited funding for training employer and employee representatives in new directions for

collective bargaining, productivity and performance measurement, and new human resource developments.

Hard Economic Bargains

We are all faced with sobering prospects on the general economic front. The scorecard for the Keynesian argument shows declining grades. Current research suggests that there is no easy equation of above average economic performance — expressed in terms of long-run employment and productivity growth — consistent with *either* Keynesian, egalitarian solutions or neo-conservative, inegalitarian prescriptions (Boltho & Glyn 1995). There are currently two competing directions driving strategic economic policy choices. Either de-regulate labour markets to drive down wages in the domestic service sector to create employment — the traded sector will be largely impervious, driven, instead, by economic cycles and best practices of international competition — which will take the public sector down with it. Or, pursue tax-based, increased funding of value-added public sector services and infrastructure.

Overall, the balance of long-term economic and social advantages lie with the more interventionist policy. The major stumbling block is the acceptability to public opinion of tax increases.

This is a political issue. Society faces clear choices in response to mass unemployment. The deregulatory route implies that those groups most affected by unemployment should trade reductions in incomes and inferior conditions of work for secure jobs. By contrast, increases in tax-financed spending imply social recognition of the widespread benefits of additional employment in public services and infrastructure and willingness to bear the costs required to provide jobs under acceptable conditions. (Boltho & Glyn 1995)

If these summary economics are valid, what we now have in the provinces of Alberta and Ontario, to take two parallel examples, is Ontario's Harris and Alberta's Klein administrations pursuing the labour market de-regulation strategy with an aggressive disinterest in any associative partnership with unions, in the unfounded expectation that this will improve international competitiveness. And, particularily in Ontario, the labour movement, having rejected the previous administration's social contract restructuring offer, has mounted a political mobilization campaign in the name of a Keynesian economic assumption that has been invalidated. It is difficult to see either of these scenarios resulting in a happy ending. Declining unionization, or, at least, declining effectiveness and marginalization, emerge as default outcomes.

Politics is clearly in command on all sides. Like Don Quixote, the rider will charge off in all directions at once. For union activists, political mobilization has the appeal of an organizational-political strategy that may succeed where all else has failed. However, as the above economic discussion reveals, it is completely possible that within the de-regulated downward spiral of service industries, unionists' energies will be completely consumed by the distributional struggles that swallowed a generation of private sector unionists before them.

What's missing is a new strategic bargaining strategy. For the remainder of the decade, public sector bargainers will search for a new strategy on the difficult terrain of the new public sector economics. With many Canadian administrations — Klein in Alberta and Harris in Ontario leading the way — firmly committed to de-regulating public sector labour markets and downward movement of wages, it is difficult to see public sector Wagnerism sustaining itself in the future. If it does, the consequences will likely be short-lived and apply to a dwindling number of services. If it doesn't, a new basis will have to be found for negotiating in the workplace that is inclusive of employees' interests, community and client needs and fiscal limits. Either way, it is a hard bargain.

APPENDICES

Appendix 1

Hospital Job Structure Data: An Analysis of Sample Collective Agreements

Collective agreements for service units in the sample hospitals were coded for the number of separate job classifications or job titles, number of employees and the weighting of seniority factors in cases of job postings and transfers. The assumption behind the analysis was that collective agreements with relatively fewer job classifications and less rigid work rules would be relatively better positioned to adapt to restructuring than more rigid traditional systems. Conversely, the presence of relative dense job structures and rigid work rules presents local parties with the opportunity to negotiate restructuring for new tradeoffs, such as extension of new forms of employment security and training opportunities, in exchange for greater job class and work rule flexibility.

Table 1

Hospital	Union Contract	Number of Employees	Number of Classifications	Seniority Factors
H4	CUPE 1	384	37	1
H3	CUPE 2	220	11	1
H1	CUPE 3	604	40	1
H2	SEIU 1	184	30	2

Density of Job Structures

Hospitals vary by service mixes, levels of unionization, collective agreements and number of employees per bargaining unit. However, a useful first measure which offsets relative size of hospital or size of bargaining unit, is to divide the number of job classifications by the number of employees in the bargaining unit. This provides an index of Density of Job Structures. Table #2 gives the relative density of job structures for the hospitals in the sample.

Table 2: Ratio of Job Classifications to Number of Employees

Hospital	Ratio
H4	10:4
H3	20:0
H1	15:1
H2	6:1

As the table indicates, there is a considerable difference in the relative density of job structures between the comparison hospitals, even when offset for size. H3 at 1 job classification for every 20 employees is very lean, while H2 and H4 are relatively dense in this dimension. This is of course a very aggregated measure and only a rough indicator. More precise and meaningful results are given below for individual service departments.

Work Rules

Seniority rules respecting the procedures and weighting attached to seniority factors in job postings are taken as a proxy for relative rigidity of work rules. The codes assigned in Table #1 are as follows:

Seniority:
- Sole, Dominant Factor   1
- Equal Factor   2
- Applied When Others Equal   3

Where seniority is the sole or dominant factor in issues of job postings, it is ranked 1 or as a highly rigid factor. Where seniority is an equal factor it is a 2, or equal factor with ability to do the work. Where seniority is considered only after qualifications or ability to do the work are established as equal between employees it is a 3.

Taking these two measures together, job class density and seniority rules, provides a general benchmark for a hospital facing restructuring. First, the relative density of job structures indicates areas where efficiency gains could be made by consolidation of job classifications. Local labour and management parties can view this as a constraint or as an opportunity. Secondly, work rules themselves can be viewed as relatively more or less rigid, also impacting potential efficiency gains. Taken together, highly dense job classes and rigid work rules can also effect the relative ability of the hospital to adapt to rapid and dramatic changes in the fiscal environment such as severe, near-term changes to transfer payments.

Restructuring Model: H2

The picture of H2 in Table #1 may be somewhat deceiving. The hospital very recently has completed a new collective agreement with the SEIU bargaining unit which dramatically simplifies its job structure. As indicated below, H2 has consolidated eighteen traditional separate job classifications into eight consolidated job classes. The new H2 wage and job structure is presented in Table 4. Table 3 presents a traditional wage structure from one of the other hospitals in the sample. The differences are striking in the degree of change and the relative flexibility of the new H2 structure. The expected efficiency gains are obvious. Two additional points should be made. The new system was accompanied by new employment security and training commitments to employees. And, on top of the fact that H2 already had relatively more flexible seniority rules, there are implicit additional gains flowing from the fact that transfers may take place within job groups without triggering traditional job posting procedures. H2 should represent the kind of labour contract regime hospitals will move towards.

Table 3: Traditional Job Structure

Classification	Wages	Classifications	Wages
Aide	14.45	Cook 1	15.619
Dietary Helper 1	14.4	Painter	15.619
Dietary Helper 2	14.590	Baker	15.803
Technical Aide	14.766	Medical Equipment Tech	15.619
Emergency Aide	14.766	Head Cook	16.059
ECG Technician	14.766	Maint. Mechanic	16.054
Medical Equipment Aide	14.766	Journ Plumber	17.309
Dietary Helper 3	14.929	Journ Electrician	18.715
Seamstress	14.784	Journ Carpenter	18.715
Porter	14.482	Journ Air Cond/Ref	18.715
Dietary Helper (Gen.)	14.482	HNA Trainee	18.715
Morgue Attendant	14.800	HNA Experiences	14.615
Storeperson	14.800	Reg. Nursing Asst.	15.165
Laboratory Assistant	15.60	Non-Reg. Nurs. Asst.	16.012
Phlebotomist	15.607	Orthopaedic Tech.	15.584

O.R. Technician	16.050	Central Serv. Tech	16.337
Cook 2	15.441	Painter Engraver	14.454
Brush Hand Painter	15.486	Medical Equip Tech	16.993
Dispatcher	15.300	Maintenance Helper	15.619
Storekeeper	15.619	Surgical Aide	14.454
Apprentice	14.972		

Table 4: Flexible Job Structure

Group 1   14.40
Housekeeping Aide
Dietary Aide
Laboratory Aide
Supply Attendant
Patient Porter
Cleaner
Supply Attendant
Porter SPD
Non-Certified Cook
Storesman/Receiver

Group 2   14.58
Stores Receiver Maintenance
Groundskeeper Helper
NRPN
Traction Porter
Shipper/Receiver

Group 3   14.67
O.R. Instrument Supply Attendant
Therapy Aide

Group 4   15.33
Groundskeeper

Group 5   16.07
Cook

Group 6   17.48
Maintenance
Mechanic

Group 7   18.83
RPN
O.R. Technician
Carpenter
Painter
Maintenance Engineer IV

Group 8   19.60
Millwright
Maintenance Engineer III
Steamfitter
Plumber
Electrician

Analysis of Service Units

The above analysis of hospital collective agreement and work force data indicates issues of general direction but is still at a fairly high level of abstraction. More meaningful comparisons can be made by disaggregating into individual service departments. In the following tables, job structures are examined as well as relative ratios of Supervisory Density, that is the number of employees per supervisor. The assumption in the analysis is that, other things being equal, a high level of job classification per number of employees and high levels of supervisors per number of employees are indicators of economic inefficiency and relative rigidities. In the tables below, the "JC Ratio" is the number of employees per job class. High means "flat," low means "dense" layering. Super/Ratio means the number of employees per supervisor, again high means a "flat" organization, low means rigid.

Table 5: Housekeeping

Hospital	JCs	Employees	JC Ratio	Super/Ratio
H1	3	91	30.3	13
H2	1	112	112.0	37.3
H3	2	64	32.0	10.7
H4	1	98	98.0	24.5

There is significant variation in Housekeeping Departments between hospitals. H2 and H4 are very lean, as well as flat. H1 and H3 are the opposite on both measures.

Table 6: Food Services

Hospital	JCs	Employees	JC Ratio	Super/Ratio
H1	3	32	10.7	8
H2	2	93	46.5	n.a.
H3	2	38	19.0	7.6
H4	6	90	15	10.0

In Food Services, H2 is much more lean than the other hospitals. There is relative convergence in respect to levels of supervision.

Table 7: Materials Management

Hospital	JCs	Employees	JC Ratio	Super/Ratio
H1	4	9	2.3	2.3
H2	2	15	7.5	7.5
H3	2	16	8.0	16.0
H4	3	12	4.0	6.0

In Materials Management, H2 and H3 are relatively lower in job density, while H1 and H4 are significantly more dense. In levels of supervision, H1 and H3 represent relative extremes of rigid and flexible cases.

Table 8: Admitting

Hospital	JC	Employees	JC Ratio	Super/Ratio
H1	1	34	34.0	17.0
H2	2	18	9.0	18.0

The sample here is more limited, as some hospitals have decentralized their admitting function. Table #8 shows that in Admitting, H2 is relatively dense in job structures, while H1 is at the leaner end of the spectrum. The supervisory levels are the same.

Nursing: Operating Room (OR) and Emergency Room (ER)

Nursing service units are unlike others in that there is a broad, single classification of Registered Nurse, but little detail available in the aggregate data concerning specific job duties. In addition there are other bargaining unit and non-bargaining unit employees in the department. Therefore with respect to the OR and ER departments, the relevant indicators are the percentages of nursing, non-nursing and supervisory employees.

Table 9: Operating Room

Hospital	% Nurses	% Non-Nurses	% Supervisors
H1	58	40	2
H2	76	11	13
H3	78	19	3
H4	50	47	3

Table 10: Emergency Room

Hospital	% Nurses	% Non-Nurses	% Supervisors
H1	72	27	1
H2	74	24	2
H3	59	39	2
H4	64	35	1

On the face of it, there appears to be significant differences in the relative proportions of nursing to non-nursing staff in these departments, with the ORs of H1 and H4 at one end of the spectrum and H3 and H2 at the other. The H2 supervisory ratio is so significantly different that it may represent a special circumstance. In respect to ERs, there is more convergence.

Table 11: Laboratories

Hospital	JCs	Employees	JC Ratio	Super/Ratio
H1	2	83	41.5	8.3
H2	3	93	31.0	15.5
H3	2	74	37.0	12.3
H4	4	73	18.3	n.a.

In Laboratories, H1, H2 and H3 are relatively lean, while H4 is more dense in job structures. H1 is more rigid in supervision while the others are clustered at a more flexible point of convergence.

Computer Simulation of Restructuring Assumptions
Organization

The simulation model is based on a hypothetical Ontario hospital which has a direct labour wage bill of $50 million annually. In the Base Year, the hospital's budget is in balance: expenditures = revenues. In the second year, the hospital faces a twenty per cent (20%) reduction in its transfer payment revenue. The model then simulates the response of the hospital to the cuts, based on different industrial relations models.

The purpose of the simulation is not to produce exact quantitative predictions. It is meant to be a learning tool to explore different labour-management policy options and project the potential impact of different responses to hospital restructuring triggered by transfer payment reductions.

Industrial Relations Model: Traditional vs. Mutual Gains/Patient-Centred Care

Two different models of labour-management relations are used in the simulation. The first Traditional Model is characterized by traditional adversarial industrial relations where union and management are very arms length, they have a very traditional collective agreement with job structures and work rules. The second example is a Mutual Gains Model with the kind of employee involvement, simplified job structures and work rules like H2, multi-skilling, employee and union involvement associated with a patient-centred care approach to service delivery.

Scenarios

Both models use the same economic assumptions: a $50 million direct labour cost and a twenty per cent (20%) reduction in transfer payments. In the Traditional Model, there is no fundamental change to the labour-management approach and nothing is changed in the collective agreement. In the case of the Mutual Gains Model, the parties bargain a package that includes accelerated early retirement and an employment security agreement for permanent full-time employees, in exchange for a major consolidation of job classifications and work rules, multi-skilling and joint productivity and service improvement committees.

Results of the Simulation

The following graphic summarizes the simulation using the impact of transfer payment changes and labour-management responses as the key indicator on the hospital operating budget.

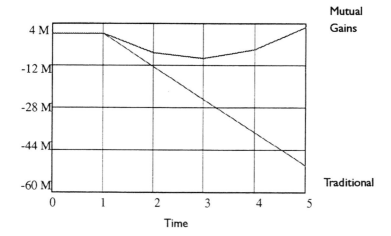

The graphic demonstrates that, in the case of the Traditional Model, the hospital faces chronic deterioration in its budgetary situation. The probable result will be major layoffs and disruptions of service. In the Mutual Gains case, the hospital is able to stabilize its finances and generate a slight surplus over time.

Appendix #2

The Ontario Ministry of Labour (MOL) Adjustment Model

Why do unions fight so strongly against job classification changes and work rule "flexibility"? Because within the present system these are the only protections against losing their jobs. When they do lose their jobs, the Ministry of Labour Adjustment Model suggests the severity of their economic losses.

Weighted Factors in MOL Labour Adjustment Model

Factor		Wage Loss	UI	Long Term UI	Early Retire
Seniority	3 yrs	$132	18.1	6	3
	4-14		23.1	10	3
	15+		26.7	15	10
Occupation	Semi-Skilled	$2,977	28.9	13	5
	Millwright	+$4,950	15.2	8	5
Education	Gr. 8	$8,693	54.8	51	8
	Primary	4,723	41.9	24	10
	Some High School	4,283	24.7	9	6
	High School	3,731	15.4	5	5
	Some College	.2,643	15.2	4	4
	College/University		13.5	6	1
Gender	Men		23.1	8	5
	Women	$2,283	21.4	13	5

Appendix 3:
Performance Indicators for U.K. Municipalities

Refuse Collection

How good is the refuse collection service?
1. The answers to these questions:
   a. Does the authority provide the containers for household waste?
   b. Does the authority provide wheeled bins for household waste?
   c. Is household waste collected from the back door of domestic properties?
   d. Is garden waste collected?
   e. Is garden waste collected free of chare?
   f. Are appointments given for the collection of bulky waste?
   g. Is bulky waste collected free of charge?
   h. Are recyclable materials collected separately from household waste?
   i. Is a direct dial telephone service available eight hours per working day and is there an answerphone service which takes messages of complaint at all other times?
   j. Are special arrangements made on request to help desabled people?
2. a. The authority's target(s) for the reliability of the household waste collection service.
   b. The performance against the target(s).
   c. The authority's target(s) for rectifying errors.
   d. The performance against the target(s).

How much does the council recycle?
3. a. The tonnes of household waste collected.
   b. The percentage of household waste recycled.

What does refuse collection cost?
4. a. The number of households.
   b. The net cost per household.

Waste Disposal

1. The amount of household waste received.

2. The percentage of household waste that was:
   a. Recyled.
   b. Incinerated with recovery of heat and power.
   c. Incinerated without recovery of heat and power.
   d. Disposed of in other ways.

What does waste disposal cost?

3. The net per tonne of household waste received.

The Provision of Social Services

How many people are given help to live in their own homes? How many are provided for in residential care?

1. a. The number of elderly people:
      (i) Aged 65-74.
      (ii) Aged 75 and over.
   b. The percentage of elderly people receiving home help or home care from the authority:
   (i) Aged 65-74.
   (ii) Aged 75 and over.
   c. The percentage of elderly people supported by the authority in residential care:
   (i) Aged 65-74.
   (ii) Aged 75 and over.
   d. The number of meals provided by the authority during the year per elderly person:
   (i) Aged 65-74.
   (ii) Aged 75 and over.
2. a. The number of adults under 65 known by the authority to have learning disabilities.
   b. The percentage of these people receiving home help or home care from the authority.
   c. The percentage of these people attending a day centre.
   d. The percentage of these people supported by the authority in residential care.
3. a. The number of adults under 65 known by the authority to have physical disabilities.
   b. The percentage of these people receiving home help or home care from the authority.

    c. The percentage of these people attending centre.
    d. The percentage of these people supported by the authority in residential care.
4. a. The number of adults aged 65 with mental problems receiving services from the local authority.
    b. The percentage of these people receiving home help or home care from the authority.
    c. The percentage of these people attending a day centre.
    d. The percentage of these people supported by the authority in residential care.
5. a. The total number of adults receiving home help or home care from the authority.
    b. The percentage of those receiving such help who receive help from the authority on:
       (i) 2-5 visits per week.
       (ii) 6 or more visits per week.

What privacy is offered to people going into residential care?

6. The percentage of adults going into residential care offered single rooms.

How many people are given an assessment of their need care?

7. a. The number of adults referred to the authority for assessment for the provision of social services.
    b. The percentage of assessments recommending.
       (i) No service.
       (ii) Service by a single agency.
       (ii) Service by more than one agency.

How long do people have to wait for equipment they need to make life easier?

8. The percentage of items of equipment costing less than £1,000 provided within three weeks of assessment.

Can those who care for others get help to take short breaks?

9. The number of nights of respite care provided or funded by the authority.

How are children looked after by the council?

10.a. The number of children being looked after by the local authority.
    b. The percentage of these children who are:

(i) In the residential accomodation.
   (ii) In foster care.
   (iii) Supported to live independently.
   (iv) Supported in other ways.
 c. The percentage of these children who moved home three times or more during the year.

How many children are placed on the child protection register?

11 a. The number of children on the protection register.
  b. The percentage of these children who have been on the register for two years or more.

How much is spent on social services?

12. The net expenditure per head of population on social services, as follows:
  a. Elderly and physical disabilities.
  b. Learning disabilities.
  c. Mental health.
  d. Children's services.
  e. Other.
  f. Total.

The Maintenance of an Adequate and Efficient Police Force

How quickly do the police answer 999 calls?

1. a. The number of 999 calls received.
   b. The local target time for answering 999 calls.
   c. The percentage of 999 calls answered within that target.

How quickly do they respond to an incident?

2. a. The local definition of "incidents requiring immediate response."
   b. The number of incidents.
   c The local target time(s) for responding to such incidents.
   d. The percentage of responses to such incidents within the target time(s).

How much crime do the police solve?

3. a. The number of recorded crimes:
     (i) Total crimes per 1,000 population.
     (ii) Violent crimes per 1,000 population.
     (iii) Burglaries of dwellings per 1,000 dwellings.

b. The percentage of crimes detected by primary and by other means (reported separately):
   (i) All crimes.
   (ii) Violent crimes.
   (iii) Burglaries of dwellings.
c. The number of crimes detected, by primary means, per officer.

How are the police tackling drunken driving?

4. a. The number of screening breath tests administerd.
   b. The percentage of such breath tests which proved poitive, or were refused by a driver.
5. a. The number of road traffic accidents involving death or personal injury.
   b. The percentage of such accidents in which at least one driver tested poitive for alcohol.

How many complaints are made against the police?

6. a. The number of complaint cases recorded from or on behalf of members of the police.
   b. The number of complaints recorded from or on behalf of members of the public.
   c. The number of such complaints substantiated.
   d. The number of such complaints resolved informally.

How many police officers are there?

7. The number of police officers available for ordinary duty per 1,000 population.

How much of their time do police officers spend in public?

8. a. The percentage of uniformed operational constables' working time spent outside the polic station and in public.
   b. The method of activity sampling used to provide this figure.

How much is spent on the police?

9. The net expenditure on police per head of population, itemised as follows:
   a. Pay and housing allowances of constables.
   b. Pay and housing allowances of ranks above constable.
   c. Pay of civilian staff.
   d. Police pensions and superannuation contributions.

e. Other costs.
f. Less governemnt grant.
g. Net cost to the authority.

Roads, Pavements and Streetlights

How many streetlights are not working?
1. a. The percentage of streetlights not working as planned.
   b. The percentage of streetlights not working as planned because they were awaiting action from the authority.
   c. The method of inspection used to monitor the above.

How quickly are dangerous potholes repaired?
2. a. The authority's definition of damage to highways which will be repaired or made safe within 24 hours.
   b. The percentage achievement within 24 hours of repairs and/or damage made safe within this category.
   c. The authority's definition of damage to pavements which will be repaired or made safe within 24 hours.
   d. The percentage achievement within 24 hours of repairs and/or damage made safe within this category.

How much does it cost to maintain the roads?
3. The cost of highway maintenance, per 100 miles ravelled by a vehicle.

What facilities are there for disabled people at pedestrian crossings?
4. The percentage of pedestrian crossings with facilities for disabled people.

Source: Audit Commission for Local Authorities and the Natural Health Service in England and Wales.

GLOSSARY

Bumping

Bumping is a procedure under collective agreements where an employee faced with layoff or displacement has a right to dislocate another employee with less service out of their job, usually subject to a qualifications and ability test. The second person can then, in turn, dislocate a more junior service person.

CAW

The Canadian Auto Workers union is comprised of approximately 270,000 members, originally in the auto industry but now a composite of transportation, general manufacturing, resource and service industry members. It is the most influential union in Canada and most vociferous defender of traditional Wagnerist approaches to collective bargaining.

CEP

The Communications, Energy and Paperworkers union is comprised of approximately 175,000 members. It is the result of the merger in the 1990s of the Communications Workers of Canada, the Energy and Chemical Workers and the Canadian Paper Workers Union. It, like the USWA, is associated with innovative approaches to collective bargaining with an emphasis on employee involvement.

The Citizen's Charter

The Citizen's Charter was introduced in the U.K. by the John Major government which set public service standards for the assessment of the quality of public services. Comparable standards have been introduced in other jurisdictions in Europe and in Australia and in a preliminary way in Alberta. The proclamation of the standards ostensibly allows the government to claim that its political obligation to provide for public services has been met without itself having managerial responsibility for actual service delivery. The Charter also changes the interface for local managers away from upward reports within the government to the external interface with the local service client-citizens.

Contract State

The Contract State is a new theory of government developed originally in New Zealand in the 1980s by radical experimentation with government downsizing and privatization. It was first introduced by the Labour government then extended by the National government. The key feature is that contracts rather than traditional budgetary and administrative rules are used to govern the delivery of public services. The change begins at the top by traditional tenured Deputy Ministers being subject to or replaced by contract executives. These executives are given a free hand to manage staff and delivery, subject to performance-based compensation and time-limited contracts.

Contracting Out

Contracting out is the removal of work that was previously performed in-house, usually under a collective agreement, performed by members of the bargaining unit. The work is either up for public tender or simply moved to another organization for implementation. The external organization is most often a private firm but can be another public community organization.

CUPE

The Canadian Union of Public Employees is the largest union in Canada with approximately 400,000 members. It was formed in the 1960s out of a merger of the National Union of Public Employees and the Canadian Union of Public Employees. Its membership is primarily in municipalities and broader public sector organizations such as hospitals, school boards and social agencies.

Decentralization

Decentralization is the movement downwards and outwards of responsibility and operations away from traditional central organizations, such as government departments and ministries, so that staff, budgets and service operations are no longer managed from the top. Often, separate operating organizations are established to manage the new operations.

Disaggregating
Disaggregating is the breaking down and separation of previously unified organizations into separate operating entities. Examples include the separation of motor vehicle licensing from an existing department of transportation and operating it as a separate agency or private organization; or, the separation of food services from regular hospital administration.

Interest Arbitration
Arbitrators usually hear and rule on disputes about rights under existing collective agreements ("rights disputes"). In most provinces, where there are restrictions on public employees' legal right to strike, interest arbitration is imposed by law so an arbitrator will hear and decide what the contract itself will contain, including wages and working conditions ("interest disputes"), which go to the economic interests of the two parties, and not just rule on what an existing contract says.

Job Control Unionism
Job control unionism is the heart of traditional Wagner-style unionism. It is characterized by narrow job titles and descriptions, rigid work rules and an active adversarial union presence on the shop floor to police employer transgressions against contract rules.

Market Mechanism
Market mechanisms in public service delivery are comprised of contract bidding or budgetary mechanisms where organizations that previously had a monopoly of service delivery or guaranteed budgets, now have to compete either with each other for contracts or against standards in order to receive their budgets.

Multi-skilling
Multi-skilling is the developing trend to have employees trained in more than one dominant skill within their job definition. For instance, in hospitals, instead of separate jobs for cleaners, dietary and laundry employees, these tasks are being combined into a patient services attendant responsible for all of the patient's physical support. Such changes usually require re-negotiating the labour contract's job titles and work rules.

Multi-tasking

Multi-tasking is the re-organizing of work so that employees are asked to now perform a variety of tasks that were previously associated with separate job definitions and job titles. It is similar to multi-skilling but often does not entail the retraining component. The economic objective is to reduce labour costs or employment.

National Labor Relations Act, 1936

The NLRA or *Wagner Act* was passed in 1936 by the U.S. Congress under the sponsorship of Senator Wagner of New York. It provided the basic framework of legal rules for labour-management relations including union recognition, separation of employer and employee interests, bargaining unit definitions and rights to strike and lock out. The basic NLRA framework was imported into Canada in the postwar period and applied in the public sector, with special provisions on strikes and arbitration in the 1960s and 1970s.

New Managerialism

The new managerialism is a recent and novel approach to the organization and operations of government and the public sector generally. The traditional approach to public administration was characterized by a strong emphasis on political responsibility of elected officials, the regulation of public services by budgetary and administrative controls. The result was a tight hierarchical bureaucracy with rigid rules and responsibilities all pointing upwards.

New Public Management

The new public management is a unique approach to organization and accountability for public service delivery. It emphasizes retention of overall budgetary and policy functions for elected public officials, but all else, including organization of delivery, compensation, service standards and employment relations is divested into the hands of professional managers. These managers act under executive, performance contracts to deliver the results but otherwise are not responsible day-to-day to the political level. Public sector managers are then free to organize services internally or to contract out.

NUPGE

The National Union of Public and General Employees is a federation of provincial government employees organizations with a membership of approximately 275,000. It represents the interests of provincial and public employees in general respecting legal, political and social policy issues but does not represent them in direct collective bargaining situations.

ONA

The Ontario Nurses Association represents 40,000 nurses in Ontario in collective bargaining. ONA emerged from the collective bargaining department of the Registered Nurses Association of Ontario, a professional nursing body, in the 1970s. ONA has effectively organized professional nurses into a highly centralized system of public sector Wagner-style unionism.

OPSEU

The Ontario Public Sector Employees Union is the second largest public sector union in Ontario with approximately 130,000 members. It emerged in the 1960s out of the previous Civil Servants Association of Ontario. It traditionally comprised members of the Ontario civil service but now half of its membership encompasses broader public sector employees such as community college and social agency employees.

Performance-based Government

Performance-based government is a new approach to public administration where public service delivery and public service managers are held accountable to outcomes and their achievement of policy objectives. Previously, traditional forms of control that relied on budget accountability and extensive manuals of administration were in use.

Public Choice Economics

Public choice economics is a conservative approach to public finance and administration. It posits that public service decision-making has been dominated by political markets in which special-interest groups and bureaucratic managers have had undue influence to the detriment of public finances and economic efficiency. Advocates suggest instead that direct economic control be given to the public through introducing economics that are more efficient and effective. A standard remedy is the introduction of a voucher system for education financing.

Purchaser/Provider Split

The purchase-provider split is the disaggregation of public service delivery where the government is the purchaser of services rather than the actual provider of the service. The original policy was developed in the U.K. with the Thatcher government's re-organization of the National Health Service. Service delivery is relegated to organizations that are either public or private community-based. These two then compete for contracts.

Regulatory Regime

A regulatory regime is the system of legal statute, regulations and voluntary agreements applying to a business, organization or employees. In the labour management arena, this includes the Labour Relations Act, Labour Standards Act on hours, vacations and working conditions, Health and Safety Act and regulations, Workers Compensation Board and collective agreement. In specific situations e.g. police and fire, other legislation and rules may also apply.

SEIU

The Service Employees International Union is an international union affiliated both to the CLC (Canadian Labour Congress) and the American AFL-CIO. It has approximately 60,000 members in Canada and competes with CUPE for employee representation in hospitals, school boards and social agencies.

Taylorist

F.W. Taylor was the leader of the industrial engineering movement at the turn of the century. He directed the re-organization of manufacturing away from traditional craft skills and towards breaking down jobs into their simplest, repetitive tasks. Labour rates could thereby be lowered, the production process speeded up and control would then be centralized in management. The same approach was later used in public administration.

Total Quality Management — TQM

Total quality management is the approach to setting quality standards and managing their measurement and implementation. This procedure is associated most closely with Edwards Deming and applied successfully by the Toyota auto company. The philosophy of TQM emphasizes quality improvement as the major source of cost and productivity improvement, and strict quality standards with constant monitoring and employee involvement.

UAW

The United Auto Workers union is one of the major private sector unions to emerge out of the mass production industries in the 1930s. Under the leadership of Walter Reuther in the 1940s and 1950s it was a major leader in the development of bargaining strategies and social-political activism in the labour movement. The Canadian Auto Workers union (CAW) emerged in the 1980s in a split within the UAW over bargaining strategies and national organizational autonomy.

UAW-Ford Windsor Strike 1945

A pivotal strike for the postwar labour-management system in Canada took place in 1945 between the UAW and Ford. It is most remembered for the union's success in gaining 'union security' (mandatory check-off of membership dues for the union by the employer) through the Rand Formula. Judge Rand acted as a mediator and composed the compromise settlement where dues would be collected for all employees covered by the labour contract, leaving them free to choose whether they would individually participate in the union's affairs. Less widely recognized, but equally important was the 1945 settlements recognition of the union on the shop floor through the shop steward and grievance system.

UFCW

The United Food and Commercial Workers union is the largest international industrial union in Canada with approximately 200,000 members. Traditionally, the union was associated with the meatpacking and retail food industries. It is now comprised of a broad range of retail and service industry members. Like USWA and

CEP it is also associated with new approaches to collective bargaining and worker retraining.

USWA

The United Steelworkers union is comprised of approximately 160,000 members, originally in the steel and mining industries but now a composite of other manufacturing and service industry members. A major influence in trade union policy circles, it is most identified with the traditional labour-NDP alliance and with new approaches to bargaining involving "worker empowerment."

Wagnerism

"Wagnerism" is the system of adversarial institutional arrangements and culture of labour-management relations that grew up in the decades after the passage of the NLRA and its Canadian counterparts. Its core is a wide divide between labour and management "sides." This is characterized in the former by narrow job definitions and rigid work rules and in the latter by aggressive management rights to unilaterally regulate investment, production, technology and work organization decisions.

Work Rule

A work rule is a provision of a collective bargaining agreement that governs how jobs are defined and what employees' rights are in seeking promotions into new jobs or remaining in jobs in the face of layoffs. Work rules also apply to scheduling of work, whether work normally performed by employees can be contracted out, and penalties on management for not adhering to the rules. Outside of these specific rules, all other decision-making is in the legal hands of management.

REFERENCES

Chapter I

Beaumont, P.B. 1995. Canadian Public Sector Industrial Relations in a Wider Setting Gene Swimmer and Mark Thompson eds. *Public Sector Collective Bargaining in Canada*, Kingston: IRC Press.

Canadian Union of Public Employees, 1994. *The Best Defence: How to Plan for Workplace Restructuring*, Ottawa.

Gunderson, M. and D. Hyatt. 1996. The Cost of Doing Nothing: Why An Active Labour Adjustment Strategy Makes Sense in Ontario's Health Sector. Ontario Health Sector Training and Adjustment Panel. Toronto.

Gunderson, Morley. 1995. Public Sector Compensation. Swimmer and Thompson eds. *Public Sector Collective Bargaining in Canada*, Kingston: IRC Press.

Gunderson, Morley, R. Hebdon and Hyatt. 1996 Collective Bargaining in the Public Sector *American Economic Review*, Vol. 86, No. 1, March: 315-326.

Gunderson, Morley and F. Reid. Public Sector Strikes in Canada. Swimmer and Thompson eds. *Public Sector Collective Bargaining in Canada*, Kingston: IRC Press.

Hebert, Gerard. 1995. Public Sector Bargaining in Quebec: The Rise and Fall of Centralization. Swimmer and Thompson eds. *Public Sector Collective Bargaining in Canada*, Kingston: IRC Press.

Kumar, Pradeep. 1995. Canadian Labour's Response to Work Reorganization. *Economic and Industrial Democracy*, Vol. 16, Number 1, February.

National Union of Public and General Employees. 1994. *Negotiating Quality Public Service*. Ottawa; December.

O'Grady, John. 1992. Arbitration and Its Ills. Queen's University, Mimeo.

Rose, Joseph B. 1995. The Evolution of Public Sector Unionism. Swimmer and Thompson eds. *Public Sector Collective Bargaining in Canada*, Kingston: IRC Press.

Stoddard, Jarvenpaa and Littlejohn. The Reality of Business Process Reengineering: Pacific Bell's Provisioning Process. *California Management Review*, Vol. 38, No. 3, Spring 1996, 57-76.

Swimmer, Gene and Thompson eds. 1995. *Public Sector Collective Bargaining in Canada*, Kingston: IRC Press.

Chapter 2

Armstrong. 1995. The Health Reform Agenda and Industrial Relations under Canadian Social Democratic Regimes. Ontario Federation of Labour, Health Research Project Working Study Series. Toronto.

Barzelay, M. 1992. *Breaking through Bureaucracy: A New Vision for Managing in Government*. Berkely, CA: University of California.

Borins. The New Public Management is Here to Stay. *Canadian Public Administration*. 38, 1:122-132.

_____. 1995b. A Last Word. *Canadian Public Administration*. 38: 1:137-138.

_____. 1994a. Public Sector Innovation: Its Contribution to Canadian Competitiveness. Kingston: *Government and Competitiveness*, School of Policy Studies, Queen's University.

_____. 1994b. Government in Transition: A New Paradigm in Public Administration. A Report on the Inaugural Conference of Commonwealth Association for Public Administration and Management. Toronto: CAPAM.

Bovaird, Tony. 1996 Performance Assessment of Service Quality: Lessons From U.K. National Initiatives to Influence Local Government. Hill, Klages, Loffler eds. *Quality, Innovation and Measurement in the Public Sector*, New York: Peter Lang.

Cuttance, Peter. Building High Performance School Systems, Keynote Address to the Eighth International Congress for School Effectiveness and Improvement. Leewarden, The Netherlands. January 3-6.

Denhardt, R.B. 1993. *The Pursuit of Significance: Strategies for Managerial Success in Public Organizations*, Belmont, CA: Wadsworth.

GAO 1996. Managing for Results: Steps Congress Can Take to Foster Aggressive GPRA Implementation. Statement of Charles A. Bowsher, Comptroller General of the United States. Washington, D.C.: United States General Accounting Office.

Hebdon, Robert. 1994. *The Perils of Privatization: Lessons for New York State*, December.

Hill, Hermann, Klages, Loffler eds. 1996. *Quality, Innovation and Measurement in the Public Sector*. New York: Peter Lang

Joint Policy and Planning Committee. Proposal for a Rate-Based Funding Approach. August 4, 1994, 15-16.

Jorgensen and Beck. 1996. Rescuing Public Services: On the Tasks of Public Organization in Hill, Klages, Loffler eds. *Quality, Innovation and Measurement in the Public Sector.* New York: Peter Lang

Klages, Helmut and Masser. Ratios and Indicators as a New and Essential Part of Present Administrative Reform. Hill, Klages, Loffler eds. *Quality, Innovation and Measurement in the Public Sector*, New York: Peter Lang.

Loffler, Elke. A Survey on Public Sector Benchmarking Concepts. Hill, Klages, Loffler eds. *Quality, Innovation and Measurement in the Public Sector*, New York: Peter Lang.

Mustonen, Maili. 1996. The ISO 9000 Pilot Project: Trial of the Applicability of an ISO 9000 Quality Management System in Five Municipal Service Functions in Finland. Hill, Klages, Loffler eds. *Quality, Innovation and Measurement in the Public Sector.* New York: Peter Lang.

OECD. *Using Performance Measures in Government.* Paris 13 Nov 1995. PUMA/PAC (95)

Oregon Benchmarks: Standards for Measuring Statewide Progress And Institutional Performance. Oregon Progress Board. December 1994.

Osborne, D. and T. Gaebler. (1992). *Reinventing Government: How the Entrepreneurial Spirit is Transforming the Public Sector.* Reading, MA: Addison-Wesley.

Pollitt, Christopher. 1996. Management Techniques for the Public Sector: Pulpit and Practice. Hill, Klages, Loffler eds. *Quality, Innovation and Measurement in the Public Sector.* New York: Peter Lang.

Savoie, Donald J. 1995a. What is Wrong with the New Public Management? *Canadian Public Administration.* 38.

_____. 1995b. Just Another Voice From the Pulpit. *Canadian Public Administration.* 38.

Walsh, Kieron. *Public Services and Market Mechanisms: Competition, Contracting and the New Public Management.*

Chapter 3

Green, Roy. 1995. Measuring Performance in Health Care. Employment Studies Centre. University of Newcastle, Australia Mimeo. May.

Haiven, Larry. 1995. Industrial Relations in Health Care: Regulation, Conflict and Transition to the 'Wellness Model.' Gene Swimmer and Mark Thompson eds. *Public Sector Collective Bargaining in Canada*, Kingston: IRC Press.

Harrison, Stephen and Christopher Pollitt. 1994. *Controlling Health Professionals*. Open University Press. Buckingham.

Ministry of Health. 1993. Funding Reallocation for Fiscal 1994/95: A policy discussion paper. Hospital Funding Committee of the JPPC. Toronto July 12.

Ministry of Health. 1994. Funding Reallocation for Fiscal 1994/95: Results of Regional Consultations and Hospital Funding Committee Recommendations. Hospital Funding Committee of the JPPC. Toronto January 7.

Ministry of Health. 1995. Joint Policy and Planning Committee, Proposal for a Rate-Based Funding Approach. Toronto. August 4.

Pollitt, Christopher. 1995 Justification by Works or by Faith? *Evaluation*. Vol. 1(2).

Trerise, Barbara and Louise Lemieux-Charles. 1994. A Study of the Multiskilled Service Assistant Role at the Sunnybrook Health Science Centre. University of Toronto: December.

Sunnybrook Health Science Centre. 1995. *Creating a Multiskilled Position*. Toronto.

Sunnybrook Health Science Centre. 1995. *Skill Set for Patient-Focused Care*. Toronto.

University Hospital. 1994. *Creating Our Future: Business Case for Re-Engineering the Work Force*. London, Ontario Feb. 18.

Warrian, Peter. 1995 Performance Indicators and the Budget Process: The Ontario Hospitals Reallocation Formula. Paper presented at IIAS Workshop on Public Sector Productivity and Performance Measurement. Perth March 8-9.

Chapter 4

AFL-CIO. *Excellence in Public Service*.

Alford, J. and O'Neill, D. 1994. *The Contract State*. Deakin University Press: Victoria.

American Public Welfare Association. 1994. *JOBS: Measuring Client Success*. Washington.

Canada. Department of Finance. 1995. *Budget Plan*. Ottawa February 28.

Donaldson, L. 1990. The Ethereal Hand: Organizational Economics and Management Theory. *Academy of Management Review*. 15(3).

Eaton and Voos, Graham, Katherine. 1995. Collective Bargaining in the Municipal Sector. Swimmer and Thompson eds. *Public Sector Collective Bargaining in Canada*. Kingston: IRC Press.

Halachmi. 1995. Re-engineering and public management: some issues and considerations. *International Review of Administrative Sciences*, Vol.61, 329-341.

Howard, M. 1991. Effectiveness and Quality of Service Data: Public Sector "Affluence," Private Sector "Squalor"? *Australian Journal of Public Administration.* (50)3, 264-273.

Jackson, Richard L. 1995. Police and Firefighter Labour Relations in Canada. Gene Swimmer and Mark Thompson eds. *Public Sector Collective Bargaining in Canada.* Kingston: IRC Press.

Jensen, M.C. & W.H. Meckling. 1976. Theory of the firm: Managerial behaviour, agency costs and ownership structures. *Journal of Financial Economics*, Vol. 3, 305-3260.

Marsden, D. and Momigliano, S. 1995. Economic theory of incentives and its implications for the design of public service performance related pay schemes. Paper presented at the 10th World Congress of the International Industrial Relations Association. Washington 31 May-4 June.

McGuire, L. 1994. Service Delivery Agreements: Experimenting with Casemix Funding and 'Schools of the Future'. John Alford & Deirdre O'Neill. *The Contract State.* Deakin University Press.

Moe, T. 1984. The New Economics of Organization. *American Journal of Political Science. 28, 739-775.*

Municipality of Metropolitan Toronto. 1995 Social Services Division. *From Income Support to Independence.* Toronto.

Municipality of Metropolitan Toronto. *Performance Measures in Social Services Delivery.* Toronto.

Neelen, G.H.J.M., 1993. *Principal-Agent Relations in non-profit organizations.* Universiteit Twente. Enschede Netherlands.

Prager, Jonas. 1994. Contracting-Out: Theory and Policy. *International Journal of Law and Politics.* Vol. 25.

Savas, Emmanuel. 1992 Privatization and Productivity. Marc Holzer ed. *Public Productivity Handbook.* Marcel Dekker: New York.

Spice, J. 1993. Service Quality Standards: A Canadian Perspective. *Canberra Bulletin of Public Administration.* No. 74.

Stewart, J. and Walsh, K. 1992. Changes in the Management of Public Services. *Public Administration.* Vol. 70, Winter.

Weller, P., Gardner, M., Stevens, B. 1993. The Role of the Public Sector: Implications for the Australian Public Service. *Canberra Bulletin of Public Administration.* No. 72, April, 1-23.

Chapter 5

Canadian Union of Public Employees — CLC, Local 1000. 1996. *Collective Agreement Between Ontario Hydro and Power Worker's Union.* April 1, 1994-March 31.

Electricity Commission of New South Wales. 1990. *The Future: The Electricity Commissions T.E.A.M. Plan Implementation.* Sydney. April.

Haddad, Carol. 1995. *Sectoral Training Partnerships in Canada: Building Consensus Through Policy and Practice.* Eastern Michigan University. Ypsilanti. February.

Hirsh, Richard. 1990. Regulation and Technology in the Electric Utility Industry: A Historical Analysis of Interdependence and Change. Jack High ed. *Regulation: Economic Theory and History.* Ann Arbor. University of Michigan Press.

Ichniowski, Casey, Kathryn Shaw and Giovanni Prennushi. 1993. The Effects of Human Resource Management Practices on Productivity. Carnegie Mellon University, Mimeo. August.

PWU. May 6, 199.

Ontario Hydro. 1994. Corporate Compensation and Benefits Division. *Memorandum on VRP Statistics.* November 17.

Ontario Ministry of Labour, Economics and Labour Market Research. 1993. *The Displaced Workers of Ontario: How Do They Fare?* Toronto.

Reich, Robert. 1996. *The Work of Nations.* New York.

Verma, Anil & Cutcher-Gershenfeld. 1993. Joint Governance in the Workplace: Beyond Union-Management Cooperation and Worker Participation. Kaufman, B.E. and Kleiner, M.M. eds. *Employee Representation: Alternatives and Future Directions.* Madison, Wisconsin: Industrial Relations Research Association.

Chapter 6

Boltho, Andrea and Andrew Glyn. 1995. Can macroeconomic policies raise employment? *International Labour Review.* Vol. 134, No.4-5.

Bowles, Samuel and Herbert Gintis. 1995. Productivity-enhancing egalitarian policies. *International Labour Review.* Vol. 134, No.4-5.

Boyer, Robert. 1995. The Future of Unions: Is the Anglo-Saxon Model a Fatality, or Will Contrasting National Trajectories Persist. *British Journal of Industrial Relations.* 33:4 December.

Cohen, Steven and William Eimicke. 1996. Understanding and Applying Innovation Strategies in the Public Sector. Paper presented to 57th

Annual National Conference of the American Society for Public Administration. June 29-July 3, Atlanta, Georgia.

Freeman, Richard. 1995. The Future for Unions in Decentralized Collective Bargaining Systems: US and UK Unionism in an Era of Crisis. *British Journal of Industrial Relations.* 33:4 December.

Graham, Clive. 1994. Towards Best Practice: A Strategic Approach to Agenda Setting in Public Sector Enterprise Agreements. *Management.* April. 17-21.

Johnson, David. 1996. Statement to the Legislature: Interim Report on Business Planning and Cost-Savings Measures. Queens Park. Toronto. April 11.

OPSEU. 1996. What's in the Deal? Toronto. March 29.

New South Wales Government. Delivering Better Service: Progress and Achievements in Public Sector Reform in New South Wales. 1988-1994.